NOT OUT
AT CLOSE
OF PLAY

NOT OUT
AT CLOSE
OF PLAY
A LIFE IN CRICKET

DENNIS
AMISS
WITH JAMES GRAHAM-BROWN

Jacket illustration: Ken Kelly/Popperfoto via Getty Images.

First published 2021

The History Press
97 St George's Place, Cheltenham,
Gloucestershire, GL50 3QB
www.thehistorypress.co.uk

British Library Cataloguing in Publication Data.
A catalogue record for this book is available from the British Library.

ISBN 978 0 7509 9245 9

Typesetting and origination by The History Press
Printed by TJ Books Limited, Padstow, Cornwall

Contents

Foreword
By Sir Geoffrey Boycott

I have had the pleasure of opening the batting with Dennis for England and playing against him for Yorkshire. Underneath that mild-mannered exterior was a tough, determined, high-quality batsman. His record for England and Warwickshire is excellent. Batting at the other end, I was in the best position to observe and, let me tell you, Dennis was a top player.

In 1974 his score of 262 not out in the second innings of the Second Test in Jamaica against the West Indies was outstanding. It was this major contribution that got England a draw as the rest of the side put together made only 129 runs.

For me, his finest moment, and one of the greatest innings I have seen, was his 203 at the Oval versus the West Indies in 1976. Dennis had been overlooked by the selectors for the first four Tests and, when he got the call, England were already 2–0 down and had lost the series, having been pummelled by their fast-bowling attack.

Dennis was mainly a front-foot batsman – which is not an ideal way to take on the 'quicks'. He knew he would be tested by a lot of short stuff, so he cleverly changed his technique. Doing that overnight is very, very difficult – but needs must! Just before the fast bowlers delivered the ball, he went back and across his stumps to be in a better position to handle the fast short balls. This change must have felt very awkward for him. Yet he showed great awareness of the problem and tremendous courage in the face of a very tough bowling attack: Andy Roberts,

Michael Holding and Wayne Daniel was one hell of a pace trio and bowled 70 overs in that innings.

I've always believed Test cricket is an examination of character, ability and mental toughness. For me Dennis's great innings fulfilled all those qualities.

1

Historic Hundred, Home, Hopes and High Days

It was 29 July 1986 and the minute hand on the pavilion clock at Edgbaston clicked on ominously: 4.55 p.m. and our County Championship match against Lancashire was petering out to a lifeless draw. The crowd had all gone home and it seemed inevitable that in just five minutes' time the umpires would lift the bails to signal the end of the match and leave me stranded on 84 not out – another chance to reach the elusive milestone gone.

I'd scored my ninety-ninth first-class century a few weeks before, against Glamorgan at Swansea. Since then I'd been in really good form: solid half-centuries against Derbyshire and Leicestershire and a fluent 83 against Yorkshire, but with nerves getting the better of me I hadn't been able to convert these promising starts into that all-important 100th hundred.

I don't know where it came from; I've never been one to draw attention to myself, but I just couldn't help it. The moment I'd played the last ball of Andy Hayhurst's over back up the pitch and the minute hand on the clock had moved on again, I found myself standing in front of Clive Lloyd, the Lancashire captain.

'Clive – look – I'm sorry even for asking – and I wouldn't normally – you know I wouldn't – but could we take the extra half hour? I know the match is dead and your boys have got a long drive – but – I've only got 16 to get – and this may sound selfish – and it probably is –

but – well – if I get to a hundred that would be it – 100 first-class hundreds – and I may not get another chance.'

'No worries, man,' says Clive, and off he goes to tell the umpires he's happy to play the extra half hour; he immediately summons John Abrahams, a part-time off-spinner, to have a bowl from the Pavilion end and waves to Neil Fairbrother, who hardly ever bowls, to indicate that he wants him to bowl from the other end.

Even so, with my nerves jangling at every delivery I spoon one up towards Clive Lloyd who is fielding at midwicket, but survive as he draws back from the kind of catch he would have taken easily if a result depended on it.

Eventually, I drive the ball out to deep extra cover and I've done it. I have made it to 100. After the initial elation, however, I began to question myself and the validity of the achievement. Had Clive Lloyd deliberately not gone for the catch out of kindness? Had I been unduly selfish in asking Lancashire to stay on the field? Did this century really mean anything when the match was effectively dead and there were no spectators left in the ground to witness it? All these doubts were intensified when Jamie McDowell, a member of Warwickshire's committee whom I really respected and who had stayed till the end of the day's play, came up to me in the bar.

'Well done, Dennis,' he said, and then added, 'but I'm not really sure that's the right way to do it.'

I'd been planning to retire at the end of the season but now I began to think that perhaps I should play on for another and score a century without the collusion of the opposition. Yes – I'd battled to 84 against a strong attack and every one of those runs was as hard-earned as any I'd scored in my career, but I couldn't ignore those last few that had got me over the line; they felt phoney somehow and I wanted to do it properly.

Set against that, though, was the plain and simple fact: I was 43 years old, and playing on for yet another season might have been interpreted as me putting my own interests before those of the team and the club, which had been such an important part of my life for as long as I could remember.

★

Perhaps it was destiny that Edgbaston became my 'home from home' as I was born on 7 April 1943 in Harborne, no more than ten minutes' walk from the ground. My first connection with cricket began that very day when my parents named me Dennis Leslie after the Compton brothers: Denis, who had already won fame in the 1930s as Middlesex and England's most dashingly fluent and prolific batsman, and Leslie, who kept wicket for Middlesex but won greater fame as a member of the mighty Arsenal football side.

The Second World War was still raging and while I obviously have no memories of those very early days, the legacy of the war would play a very significant part in my upbringing and in my development as a cricketer. My father, Vic, had served as an air-raid warden during the Birmingham Blitz, which lasted from August 1940 to April 1943. In that time Birmingham became the third most heavily bombed city in the UK (behind London and Liverpool), suffering as nearly 2,000 tons of explosives were dropped on it.

Dad was a good cricketer who had been good enough to take 6 wickets in 6 balls in a club match against one of the better local sides, and when peace came he, like so many of his generation, set about making up for all the matches missed. In addition to playing for the Birmingham Cooperative Society Cricket Club on Saturdays, he founded his own Sunday side in honour of his brave wartime colleagues which he called HARPS, an acronym for the Honorary Air Raid Precaution Services.

HARPS was a nomadic team which played against some of the best clubs in the West Midlands. The standard was high and, alongside the ex-air-raid wardens, Dad was able to call on players from Birmingham League senior sides including the fast bowler 'Butch' White who went on to play so successfully for Hampshire and England.

Growing up with a father who played highly competitive cricket every Saturday and Sunday from the beginning of April through to the end of September laid the foundations for my own love affair with the game. Looking back, though, I can see that of equal significance was the deeply rooted connection between cricket and family life. The Amiss annual summer holiday was a clear illustration of this: every August throughout my childhood we spent a glorious fortnight in a friend's caravan in Barmouth on the Welsh coast. The beaches were magnificent and once the tide went out we were left with the best solid sand cricket pitches imaginable. Every single day, rain or shine, Dad, my brother Alan and I played cricket for hours on end.

The point was, of course, that, just as the war had reduced community engagement in sport and leisure, it had also limited opportunities for family activities, but as far as my dad was concerned these precious moments were not be confined to a fortnight in August. Thus it was that every Sunday throughout the summer, when Dad was playing cricket for HARPS, he took us all with him – my mum, me and my brother – and it became a tradition that all the other players also brought their families along with them. We'd all board a coach rammed to the gunnels with picnic hampers, blankets and deck chairs and off we'd go for a day full of laughter, singing and, above all, a tremendous feeling of adventure. These joyous Sunday outings played a formative role in shaping my cricketing philosophy that the game cannot be defined simply by runs scored or wickets taken, and that the joy in being a cricketer extends way beyond the hours of play.

It is perhaps because of this that when I look back on my playing days, my memory of personal statistics is decidedly hazy, and yet the evenings I spent with cricketing friends and their families, the many fascinating places throughout the world that we visited together, the experiences, jokes and stories that we shared, are all as vivid as if they happened yesterday.

That is not to say that personal performance was not important to me. From the moment I first picked up a cricket bat all I wanted to do was score as many runs as humanly possible. It was because of this that I had such a commitment to practice and to tinkering endlessly with my grip and stance as I searched in vain for the technical perfection that is a batsman's holy grail.

From the age of 7, every moment of every summer day when I wasn't at school was devoted to becoming my hero Denis Compton, after whom I had been named. The only problem for me and my small group of young cricketing friends was finding somewhere to play. Our favoured location was the Birmingham Cooperative Society Sports Club, where my dad played cricket on Saturdays – the club had extensive grounds including tennis courts, a bowling green and a huge cricket ground with an outfield that was flat and true, and it was the perfect place for a small boy to practise his batting. The only problem was Freddie Pitt, the groundsman, who guarded the field like the crown jewels. No matter how close we kept to the outer edge or how far we were from the hallowed square, the moment Freddie spotted us he was out of his shed, onto his bicycle and hurtling towards us. 'You boys get off my field,' he'd yell. 'Do you hear me – off my field – I've told you before and I'll tell you again – if I see you on my precious field again I'll tell your dads – and you'll get a right walloping – do you hear me? Off my field!'

Off we'd run before he got to us and we'd disappear behind the nearest tree, bush or fence and wait for him to cycle slowly back to his shed before moving our game to an even more distant location. Half an hour later out he'd be out again on his bicycle, legs going like bees' wings, yelling as he pedalled. And so it went on until we'd all had enough for the day and packed up to go home.

If we felt we'd tested Freddie's patience enough we'd put our visits to his precious field on hold for a few days. This didn't mean the end of playing cricket – most certainly not. These were the very early 1950s and because there was still post-war rationing we had all learned how to 'make do' and improvise with very little. Thus it was that a 22-yard stretch of tarmacked street just outside number 40 Sunnymead Road, Yardley, where I lived, became our cricket pitch, and the T-junction sign at one end became a highly effective makeshift wicket.

The only difference between the matches played here and those we enjoyed at the Cooperative Society ground was that the 'street cricket' attracted some of the older boys in the neighbourhood. This meant that the competition intensified considerably, and so, at the age of just 7, I found myself batting against 11- and 12-year-old lads who made no concessions whatever to my size or age. The fact that my fast-bowling brother Alan was one of the older boys who joined in, and that we were never on the same side, added a distinctly personal dimension to the proceedings. I relished the challenge and it became a matter of honour not to be bowled out by Alan.

No helmets, no gloves, no pads and no adult supervision; all we had to rely on for protection was our own skill, our own nerve and determination. It was in many ways a great way to start learning the game and I believe now that facing my big brother and his even bigger friends as they hurled the ball down as fast as they could at me on the street's hard surface sharpened my competitive edge and my drive to succeed against the odds. I am also clear that without the lessons I learned from these early skirmishes I would never have made the comeback that I did against the ferocious pace and hostility of the West Indian fast bowlers in 1976.

There were those times, of course, when none of my friends were able to play with me and I was left to my own devices. It was on these occasions that I took on the persona of Tony Lock, bowling my slow left-arm spinners against the coalhouse wall on which three stumps had been painted. Ball after ball thumped into the wall as Tony Lock ran through the opposition, maintaining a perfectly straight bowling arm, perhaps for the first time in his career!

The summer of 1953 was a watershed moment in my cricketing development. This was when a brand-new mahogany box set television was first introduced into the Amiss household. It turned up just in time for the arrival of Lindsay Hassett's formidable Australian touring side.

By this stage in my life both my parents were well aware that there was little or nothing that could get me away from cricket matches in the street or from bowling for hours on end at the coalhouse door. That summer, though, all they had to do was call out, 'I don't know if you're interested, son, but Denis Compton's in,' and I was into the house in a flash, glued to the screen as my hero took on Lindwall and Miller at Lord's, scoring a thrilling 57. I was equally spellbound a few days later as Compton once again held the England innings together at Old Trafford, falling just a few runs short of another half-century, and again the following week when he launched a brilliant counter-attack at Headingley, making a glorious 61 to ensure England drew a match that they seemed certain to lose.

Another significant factor in my early cricketing development was my schooling. These were the days of selective education with the 11+ examination determining whether you went to one of Birmingham's prestigious grammar schools or to the local secondary modern school, with failure meaning a drastic reduction in future career options. While it was perfectly clear from my early school days as a pupil at Church Road Primary in Yardley that my academic prowess was decidedly limited, I was nonetheless incredibly fortunate that Mr John Wright, one of the teachers, took me under his wing. A keen club cricketer himself, John devoted hours of his time during the lunch break and after school to supervising cricket practice in the summer and football training in the winter months. Always encouraging and supportive, he played a critical role in making my days at primary school happy, purposeful and fulfilling.

As anticipated, in September 1954, aged 11 years and 5 months, I went on to Oldknow Road Secondary Modern School in Small Heath. The fact that I cannot recall a single lesson during the four and a half years that I spent at the school is a pretty good indication that I was not grammar-school material. What's more, I feel no resentment now, any more than I did all those years ago, that I was consigned to what most people regarded as an inferior education.

David Brown, one of my oldest and closest friends from my days at Warwickshire, has always maintained that I am the most stubborn man he has ever met. There may well be truth in what he says because, if anything, failing the 11+ made me even more determined to prove my worth and develop the talent for batting that I appeared to have been born with.

These days I am often asked where my drive to succeed in the face of adversity came from. On reflection I think that it probably has its roots in the rather romanticised version of British heroism that was prevalent in the post-war era. Most of the British boys' adventure stories and action films of the period told the stories of the indomitable spirit of men like Douglas Bader in *Reach for The Sky* and Guy Gibson in *The Dambusters*. It was their 'never-say-die' attitude that enabled them to win through in the end against seemingly overwhelming odds.

It was a quality that my dad certainly tried to instill in me when, at the tender age of 9, my trial to be part of a youth coaching scheme run by Warwickshire County Cricket Club ended in disappointment. It was 1952 and the coaches responsible for selecting the elite squad felt that I was not ready for the intensive training that they offered every Saturday morning in the indoor school at Edgbaston.

It was a far greater blow than my subsequent failing of the 11+ exam, but, far from being discouraged by the rejection, it proved to be the stimulus that I needed. For the next twelve months I practised my batting at every opportunity wherever and whenever I could; hours were spent in front of the bedroom mirror at home checking my stance, my grip and my pick-up before presenting myself at Edgbaston a year later for my second trial. This time the coaches all agreed that I was ready and so, while I may not have made it to grammar school, every Saturday morning for the next five years I went to the indoor school at Edgbaston to work on my game, guided every step of the way by Derief Taylor and Ernest 'Tiger' Smith, Warwickshire County Cricket Club's most experienced coaches.

My story, however, is not one of those rags-to-riches blockbusters in which the main character has a meteoric rise to fame and fortune; my progress through the ranks was more measured and gradual. Little by little the coaching that I received at Edgbaston began to have a positive effect on my game, and I became known locally as a schoolboy player of some promise.

I took another step forward when I began playing men's cricket for the Birmingham Cooperative 2nd XI at just 13 years of age. One of my first matches was against a Walsall club side and I came to the wicket at no. 10 with my team facing a heavy defeat. Somehow I managed to frustrate the opposition with a dogged display of defence, ending up with a hard-fought and obdurate 30 not out, which was more indicative of a steadiness of temperament than precocious talent.

Suffice it to say that I never scored a century in the Birmingham league nor in a school match prior to signing with Warwickshire. I did, however, have moments suggesting that I was not one to be daunted by the big occasion. In 1957, for example, I represented my school against Kings Norton in the semi-final of the Docker Shield, which was a knockout competition involving all the Birmingham schools. I scored a half-century in our innings as we posted a total of 154. In reply Kings Norton had got to 128–9, but with night drawing in and the light failing there was a real danger that there would have to be a replay. Indeed, as the clock edged towards 8.30 p.m. the umpires informed us that there would be one more over. As captain, I had no doubt who should bowl it; with my third ball I knocked back the Kings Norton batsman's off stump and we had made it to the final.

The Docker Shield final versus Wheeleys Road School was to be played at Edgbaston, and I remember the immense pride I felt as once again I got to 50 and raised my bat towards my mum and dad sitting in the stand. A few minutes later the runs I had scored counted for nothing; the heavens opened and the match had to be abandoned due to a waterlogged pitch. To add insult to injury we were told that the replay the following week would not be played on the county ground but at Mitchell and Butlers Cricket Club.

I went home that night totally deflated and convinced that all my efforts had been for nothing. A good night's sleep, however, has always been the best tonic for me and the following day the stubborn streak that had been sidelined for a night raised its dogged head. 'Come on, Dennis,' I said to myself, 'you've done it once and you can do it again.'

Over the course of the next few days I kept repeating those same words over and over again. At some point I must have started believing my own propaganda, because when the replay came not only did I score another half-century but we won the match convincingly. Lifting the Docker Shield as captain of the Oldknow Road Secondary Modern School cricket team was a very proud moment which more than compensated for the previous doubts and disappointments.

That year, 1957, was not only my final year of school but it was also the last cricket season that I would play as an amateur. Successes at a local level had earned me selection for the Birmingham Boys side against the Southern Schools at Basingstoke and on a blazing hot August day I scored yet another 50 in an innings that showed me that I was capable of competing at more than a local level. Perhaps it was also the reason that just a few weeks later, Leslie Deakins phoned to offer me a contract to join Warwickshire County Cricket Club for the 1958 season at the princely salary of £150 per annum.

2

Nursery, Nerves and Noughts

Almost since I could walk, Edgbaston had been my second home; it was where I had come every week from the age of 10 for coaching, where I had spent countless long summer days watching Eric Hollies bamboozle opposition batsmen, or Tom Dollery stroke his way to yet another half-century. In spite of the fact that I knew every inch of the ground like the back of my hand, I was filled with nervous apprehension when I arrived on the morning of my 15th birthday – 7 April 1958. It was my first day as a professional cricketer.

The real moment of panic came when I approached the players' entrance at the rear of the pavilion, the very spot where I had collected the autographs of so many great players over the years: Lindsay Hassett, Ray Lindwall, Keith Miller, Len Hutton, Cyril Washbrook and, of course, my one true hero – Denis Compton. How could a 15-year-old boy from Harborne presume to open the door that in my mind had always separated the gods from mere mortals like myself?

It was Tom Dollery who got me over the threshold. 'Morning, young Dennis,' he said cheerily. 'You know where the 2nd XI dressing room is – down the corridor and third on the right. Get yourself changed and wrap up warm. We don't want you pulling any muscles, especially on your first day as a professional.' And so began a seven-year apprenticeship in a game that is virtually unrecognisable from today's professional cricketing structure.

First-class cricket in the 1950s still maintained a strict hierarchical structure belonging to the Victorian age, during which cricket had developed as a professional game. Indeed, walking into the Warwickshire 2nd XI dressing room on that cold April day in 1958, it was clear that little or nothing had changed in the intervening hundred years. Cricketers were still divided by the class-based distinction of amateur or professional, which finally came to an end in 1963. Amateur players included our own MJK Smith, along with the likes of Colin Cowdrey at Kent, Ted Dexter at Sussex and Peter May at Surrey. They had all been educated at leading British public schools and either Oxford or Cambridge where, of course, they had enjoyed three summers getting the feel of first-class cricket on flat wickets at the Parks or Fenners.

The main qualification for amateur or 'gentleman' status was to play the game without any financial remuneration. Curiously, in the mind of the great British sporting public this apparently selfless act afforded the amateurs a higher moral status. While the paid professionals treated the game as no different from any other job for which payment was appropriate, the amateurs were perceived as aspiring to the Corinthian ideal of playing the sport for its own sake. The truth was that the amateur/professional categorisation was riven with hypocrisy and the vast majority of players purporting to be amateurs were paid for their services in indirect ways, either through thinly veiled expenses schemes or by payment for executive roles that didn't require the incumbent to turn up for work.

When I joined Warwickshire in 1958, the amateur and professional classification was still clearly evident and symbolised by the fact that there was a separate dressing room for the 'gentlemen'. In addition, there was a further stratification in the hierarchy between those of us who had the status of professionals in that the 'capped' and 'uncapped' players also changed in different rooms. What's more, the delineations of status were rigidly enforced and as 'uncapped' junior players we were expected to knock on the door of the 1st XI dressing room and wait for permission to enter.

The whole system was designed on an archaic concept of deference, reinforcing the idea that young players should 'know their place' and 'wait their turn'. If the demarcation lines of the dressing rooms did not deliver this message then the football sessions played in the pavilion car park as part of pre-season training most certainly did. Many's the time that Jim Stewart flattened me onto the tarmac with challenges that would get the red card from even the most liberal of premiership referees. There was never a word of apology nor the offer of a hand to help me up from the hard surface even though on one occasion it was clear I had really damaged my knees. Even so, the relish he and one or two of the other senior players got from reminding us of where we stood in the pecking order was all too clear.

Brought up in the era of compulsory National Service, Jim regarded the junior players as spoilt brats who needed toughening up. He would often berate us for the fact that we lacked the discipline that he believed came with two years in the army. 'A couple of months with a good sergeant major, that's what you lot need; learn to follow orders without question; keep you in place; stop you getting above yourselves.'

It was a far cry from the modern game with its emphasis on nurturing young talent through a whole network of support including agents, coaches, dieticians and psychologists. The attitude towards young players in 1958 was far more brutal and unforgiving, and yet in a curious way it may have been a better preparation for the painful reality of the life I discovered as a professional batsman at the highest level. Indeed, when Michael Holding, Dennis Lillee or Jeff Thomson is about to release the ball at your head at 90+ miles per hour you only have yourself to rely on.

In fact, as I look back on those early days over fifty years later I am in many ways grateful to the likes of Jim Stewart for toughening me up in the only way that they knew how – the way that it had been done to them in their formative years. That is not to say that I have a nostalgic longing, as many do, for the game to revert to the kind of cricket that was played in those days: seventeen first-class counties playing thirty-two three-day matches in an endless routine: two matches per week throughout the season with only Sundays off; no one-day competition of any kind; only one division; no relegation or promotion; no penalty for failure; no great reward for success. It had become a stale and repetitive diet, and it is no wonder that by the end of the 1950s there was a diminishing public appetite for county cricket; gate receipts were dwindling as the post-war generation found alternative entertainment at the cinema and through the increasingly popular medium of television.

Just as cricket was struggling to make its mark in 1958, so was I. The fact that there were twenty-five players on the professional staff at Warwickshire meant that even breaking into the 2nd XI was a real challenge. What's more, in my first two seasons at the club I was expected, along with the other young professionals, to sell scorecards during county matches and assist the groundsman with covers, sight screens and boundary ropes during the Test matches played at Edgbaston. In addition we had to bowl in the nets at members who were looking for practice in preparation for a club match. This was a matter of some resentment as far as I was concerned, as I reckoned the roles should have been reversed and the members should all have been bowling at me to help me prepare for my next innings.

In the midst of such tedium and frustration, I cannot begin to describe the excitement I felt when Tom Dollery told me that I would be making my debut for Warwickshire 2nd XI at Old Trafford against Lancashire 2nd XI in a two-day match beginning on 14 May 1958. The fact that it was Tom who told me of my selection was of particular significance. He had taken on the role of 2nd XI captain and coach that season, having retired the previous year from first-class cricket. He had for many years been the 1st XI captain, leading the club to the County Championship in 1951.

Realising that this was my big chance to make an early impression on one of the most influential people in the club, I devoted myself to practice as never before in the three days leading up to the fixture. Arriving at the nets before anyone else and leaving long after the others had all gone home, I persuaded anyone ready willing and able to bowl endless half-volleys at me as I sought the sweetness of touch that is indicative of being in 'good form'.

Undaunted by the overcast conditions and the presence in the Lancashire side of Colin Hilton, who had a reputation for genuine pace, Tom Dollery won the toss and elected to bat. Trying not to show my disappointment at being listed to bat at no. 8 or by the fact that we were playing on Old Trafford's Nursery Ground, I sat and watched as first Tom Cartwright and then David Ratcliffe were dismissed without a run on the board. Eric Hewitt soon followed, leaving us struggling at 3–3.

A century partnership between Chris Hawkins and Mike Youll restored the equilibrium before Mike was caught in the deep going for a big hit off the leg-spin of Brian Booth. This brought Terry Riley to the wicket who, like me, was also making his debut in a county 2nd XI match. He clipped the first ball he received off his legs towards square leg and the non-striker Chris Hawkins immediately called 'yes' and set off, before stopping mid-stride and shouting 'no'. Poor Terry was run out by at least half the length of the pitch.

This was my moment and, as Terry began the long trudge back to the pavilion, I tucked my bat under my arm and made my way to the dressing-room door where Tom Dollery was waiting to pat me on the back. 'Good luck, Dennis, and don't do anything daft. We don't want any more run-outs.'

At 147–6 our innings was in danger of falling apart, but this was my big chance to show everyone what I could do. The first ball from Brian Booth was an innocuous half-volley on leg stump and I clipped it away behind square and instantly looked up towards Chris Hawkins in anticipation of his call. 'Yes,' he yelled after a brief pause, and off I set as fast as my 15-year-old legs would carry me, desperate to get off the mark in my first big match.

'No, no,' he cried again. 'Get back, get back.'

Skidding to an unceremonious halt, I slipped and turned simultaneously before falling in an undignified heap as wicketkeeper Bill Heys gathered the ball and removed the bails.

I could only reflect on the unfairness of the game when Chris Hawkins returned to the dressing room to much back-slapping and adulation having scored 73, his highest 2nd XI Championship score up to that point. Needless to say, neither Terry Riley nor I were quite as enthusiastic about his achievement as the other members of our team!

It wasn't long before my disastrous 2nd XI debut became a source of considerable humour for the rest of the team. Indeed, a couple of weeks after the match at Old Trafford I was playing for Warwickshire Club and Ground against Birmingham Municipal on their home ground. As I came into the clubhouse bar after the match, Tom Dollery called me over to a corner of the room where team photographs and framed scorecards of old matches were on display.

'Look here, young Dennis,' said Tom, pointing to the record of a particular match. 'A.V. Amiss is your dad, isn't he?'

'Yes,' I replied. 'He used to play here.'

'Well, look what the scorecard says: "A.V. Amiss run out 0". It's hereditary, young Dennis, that's what it is. It's in the genes.'

Not surprisingly I was only selected once more for County 2nd XI Championship games during the season. It was a match against Gloucestershire 2nd XI at Ashley Down, Bristol, and in my only innings of the game I scored an inglorious 19 before being bowled attempting an expansive cover drive on a turning wicket against the future England off-spinner David Allen.

My opportunities to play in the County 2nd XI and the Minor Counties Championships were equally limited in my second season at Warwickshire and most of the cricket I played in my first two summers as a professional was limited to representing the Warwickshire Nursery XI, a side that was comprised of a combination of young professionals and trialists. Fixtures were played on Saturdays against local clubs. This meant that none of us 'young pros' were able to play in the Birmingham League, which was not only the oldest but arguably the most competitive cricket league in the country.

Fortunately, from the point of view of my cricketing development, the foolishness of this arrangement was recognised by the powers-that-be and in 1960 the Nursery XI was replaced by the Warwickshire Club and Ground XI whose fixtures were played mid-week. This meant that I was able to play for Smethwick in the Birmingham League alongside fellow Warwickshire cricketers John Jameson and Brian Richardson.

It would be hard to overstate the importance that playing league matches for Smethwick had on my development and maturity. From a cricketing point of view I would find myself batting against top-class bowlers virtually every Saturday. Dartmouth, for example, had the great leg-spinner Eric Hollies, who had taken over 2,300 first-class wickets including that of Don Bradman in his final Test match. Moseley had Bert Latham, the former Warwickshire fast bowler who had twice taken 10 wickets in an innings. They also had Ray Abell, a leg-spinner renowned for his use of the Moseley slope, while Walsall had a ferocious seamer in Gil Gregory whose accuracy was such that he seemed able to hit the famous Walsall 'ridge' at will.

While I didn't get a century in the Birmingham League before I became an established member of the Warwickshire side in 1965, the many hard-fought 50s and 60s I scored during my apprenticeship years against the likes of Moseley, Dartmouth and Walsall were fundamental in learning how to build an innings.

Perhaps even more important was the influence that playing for Smethwick had on my social and personal development. Meeting and playing with characters like Cyril Goodway and Johnny Oldham broadened my perspective of life. Cyril, who was the Smethwick captain, had played forty first-class matches for Warwickshire between 1937 and 1947. A brilliant wicketkeeper, his career had been blighted by the war and yet he never revealed a hint of bitterness or resentment. Always encouraging the younger players in the side, he was a true leader who put the spirit of the game and the unity of his team above any personal considerations.

Johnny Oldham, who had become headmaster of my old secondary school a couple of years after I left, had lived the kind of life you come across in superhero comics. He had joined the RAF as war broke out in 1939, training as a fighter pilot first on Tiger Moths and Miles Masters before moving on to the Hurricanes. Upon gaining his wings he was posted to Douglas Bader's worn-out 242 squadron towards the end of the Battle of Britain in 1940. He was then posted to fly for the RAF in Burma where he was shot down by the Japanese. He escaped capture and imprisonment by hiding in one of the most hostile jungles in the world. Astonishingly, when he emerged three months later he had a Japanese soldier in tow whom he had single-handedly taken prisoner.

What is even more remarkable is that the full details of Johnny's highly distinguished military career only became apparent when he died and obituaries appeared in local and national newspapers. The fact that I knew nothing of his wartime record when we played together for Smethwick did not in any way diminish the influence he had on my development. He lived and played his cricket as if every moment and every innings might be his last, greeting success and failure with the same broad smile and philosophical shrug of the shoulders. I can only speculate that Johnny's determination to live his life to the absolute full was out of respect for the countless number of men he had served with who had not been so fortunate.

Perhaps it was because Johnny was head of Oldknow Road Secondary School, where I had formerly been a pupil, that he took a close personal interest in me. He was particularly supportive when things were not going well and I vividly remember one occasion in the middle of a particularly bad run of form when I returned to the pavilion with yet another low score to my name.

Slumping myself down in the corner of the Smethwick dressing room and struggling to hold back the tears, I gave free rein to my feelings. 'That's it,' I announced to all and sundry. 'I'm packing up. I've had enough. That's it. I'm done.'

'Don't be ridiculous,' said Johnny, coming over and putting his reassuring hand on my shoulder. 'You can't possibly give up, not with your talent.'

'I'm not good enough and I never will be.'

'I've never heard such nonsense.'

'I can't get a run.'

'There's no such word as "can't".'

'So what do I do?'

'Keep going; keep trying; keep soldiering on; you'll get there 'cos you're made of the stuff that does, and when you do, you make damn good and sure you make the most of it. And let's have no more of this "I'm packing up" nonsense.'

Johnny taught me a lot, not least that it is impossible to achieve anything much in life without support and guidance along the way. In addition, he made me realise that if I was to achieve success as a professional sportsman I had to become far more resilient in the face of adversity. Yet he also opened my eyes to the fun that could be had not just from scoring runs but also from evenings spent with teammates sharing stories, telling jokes and enjoying each other's company.

As far as my early cricketing development at Warwickshire was concerned, my mentors were Tom Dollery, the 2nd XI captain and coach, and Tiger Smith, who ran the indoor cricket school at Edgbaston. I always felt that I had a special affinity with Tom Dollery, perhaps because he had taken on responsibility for the 2nd XI the same season that I joined the staff. To that extent he saw me as 'one of his boys' and took genuine pride in any successes that I achieved.

Having played 436 first-class games, represented England in four Test matches, and served as the captain of Warwickshire for seven seasons he knew the game inside out. He was not, however, a technical coach and at net practices he saw his role as largely organisational, making sure that all the batsmen had their twenty-minute turn at the crease. He rarely if ever offered comment and when I once sought his advice about how to improve playing the on drive, he turned it back to me: 'You can work on that tomorrow when it's your turn to bat.'

In many ways, Tom's 'work it out for yourself' approach was healthy and successful. He was never one of those meddlesome coaches who stifle flair and natural ability through dogmatic adherence to a regime that takes no account of an individual's idiosyncrasies. Nor was his style entirely laissez-faire and he was especially good at provoking thought about how to bowl at, or set a field to, a particular batsman. Because I fielded next to him in the slips I often benefited from his musings.

'Now tell me, Dennis,' he said during a match against Surrey 2nd XI when David Fletcher was cutting and pulling his way towards a half-century. 'What do you think we should do now?'

'Introduce spin into the attack, Skipper. Give the ball some air. Bowl a fuller length. Stop him using the pace of the ball.'

'Interesting thinking, young man,' he said.

The next over he reintroduced fast bowler David Brown into the attack; David Fletcher accelerated his way to an unbeaten half-century.

The fact that Tom did not always follow the advice he sought was, of course, largely irrelevant. He encouraged us to think about the game and contribute our ideas freely. To that extent he fostered a happy, open and friendly atmosphere in which humorous banter struck an easy balance with serious discussion and clarity of purpose.

Although Tom had recently retired from the first-class game, he had made his debut for Warwickshire in 1935 and as such he really belonged to an age and a culture that was entirely foreign to the young cricketers for whom he was responsible. Like so many professionals of his day, Tom had developed business interests outside the game and ran two pubs which were intended to pay for a retirement that never actually materialised. He ended up working as steward of Edgbaston Golf Club and living with Jean, his wife, in the flat above the clubhouse. His spare-time interests also reflected how much the world was changing. If the 2nd XI were playing an away match most of the young team would seek out a local pub, dance hall or cinema for an evening's entertainment. Tom, by contrast, would make his way alone to the local dog track for an evening's racing, always having a generous wad of £10 notes at the ready for a good night's betting.

On one occasion I was sitting across from him in the dressing room when he pulled out the biggest bundle of tenners I'd ever seen. 'See this, Dennis,' he said.

'You must have done well at the track last night, Tom,' I observed.

'Not just for betting, though, son. This is what I always used for a thigh pad when I was batting, especially against the real quicks – Tyson and Trueman and co. Bloody marvellous protection; I never felt a thing when I got hit.'

Tom undoubtedly came from a different era but the fact that he had little in common with any of his young charges was immaterial. What bound us together was a passionate love affair with the game of cricket and the knowledge that for all his archaic ways and eccentricities he was a kind man who wanted the very best for each and every one of us.

The man who had the biggest influence on my development as a batsman at Warwickshire was Tiger Smith. Although he had played his eleven Test matches for England before the First World War and had been born in 1886, twenty-eight years before Tom Dollery, he seemed far more in touch with the technical demands of the modern game. Thus, Tiger was the man I went to whenever I felt there was a problem with my technique.

That he was held in the highest regard by professional cricketers throughout the UK is demonstrated by the fact that Mike Brearley saw Tiger as his personal 'batting guru' and often made the journey from London to Birmingham to seek technical advice and guidance when he was out of form.

Tiger's strength as a batting coach lay in his uncanny ability to diagnose the precise cause – as opposed to the general symptoms – of any problem I was having. Whether it was a matter of balance or weight distribution at the crease, or of committing myself too early to the front foot, or a problem with my grip or pick-up, Tiger would spot it and send me off with something to work on.

This worked brilliantly for me because I always came away from a session with Tiger feeling confident that I had found a solution – and confidence was a critical issue for me. It was something that I lacked and in my early years at Warwickshire in particular I was wracked by self-doubt and the fear that I might not be good enough to build a lasting career in the game.

In this context, my relationship with Tiger Smith played a pivotal role in helping me overcome my demons. Everyone knew that he didn't waste his time on players who didn't work at their game and we also knew that he was brutally frank and honest. If he didn't think you were good enough he would tell you straight. He believed that it was kinder in the long run to face the truth, however distressing in the short term, than waste time and energy chasing dreams that were unrealistic.

The fact that Tiger was always willing to work with me was an indication that he had faith in my ability and because the advice he gave me invariably worked I came to have an unshakeable belief in his judgement. This in turn helped me to start believing in myself.

Without having achieved very much in statistical terms in my first year on the ground staff, it was with considerable trepidation that I lined up together with the other young Warwickshire professionals outside Leslie Deakins's office early one August morning to hear our fate. We had all had the same thoughts running through our minds for weeks in advance: 'Will they offer me a contract for next season?' 'What am I going to do if I'm not retained?'

In my case there was at least something to fall back on. My uncle had a flourishing tyre company where I was due to work in the winter. Although not a partner, my father was also part of the company and so I knew that even if I failed at cricket I could always join the family business on a permanent basis. Indeed, I sometimes wonder if this fall-back position gave me the security to play cricket with a little more freedom and less pressure than if it had been the be-all and end-all of life.

Nevertheless, as I lined up outside Leslie Deakins's office, the prospect of a lifetime selling tyres seemed a very poor consolation prize. I needn't have worried, however, nor indeed the following August when I went through the agonising process for a second time. On both occasions I was informed that the club had sufficient faith to retain me, increasing my salary to £175 in 1959 and to £200 in 1960.

In actual fact, my off-season work did me no end of good and when I arrived back at Edgbaston in April 1960 for my third season as a professional cricketer, although still only 17 years of age, I was far stronger and fitter from two winters of lifting an endless succession of huge lorry tyres from one enormous pile to another. I had also built up my stamina through distance running and sessions at the gym at Kynoch where Frank Mitchell, the ex-Birmingham City footballer, put me through my paces.

The 1960 pre-season practice went well and I scored runs in all of the county's warm-up matches, culminating in 110 not out for Warwickshire Club and Ground against Solihull School. In spite of the fact that my first century for a Warwickshire side was against a school attack it must have made some kind of an impression on Tom Dollery, as I now found myself a regular in the 2nd XI Championship side, having played just nine games at this level in the two previous seasons. My form was good if unspectacular: 30 not out against Derbyshire 2nd XI, followed by 21 against Northants, 26 at Leicester, and scores of 22 and 35 not out in the fixture with Surrey.

The problem was, though, that I kept finding ridiculous ways of getting out. It was particularly frustrating as on each occasion I had done the hard work and got myself settled. I was seeing the ball well; my feet were moving and I felt comfortable at the crease. So what on earth was going wrong?

'Concentration! Pure and simple, young man.' That's what Tiger Smith had to say on the subject. 'You're getting ahead of yourself. Your mind's taking you forward thirty or forty runs before you've scored them. Play the ball that's coming and don't think about anything else. And when you feel you're really in take guard and start again. It's the same when you get to a hundred – take guard and start again and get another hundred.'

This was advice that would stand me in good stead in years to come when battling against the might of the West Indies attack, but it was already embedded in my mind when I made my way to the Lockheed Sports Club, Leamington, 29 July 1960 for the beginning of our two-day 2nd XI Championship match against a Nottinghamshire side that included the Jamaican-born fast bowler Carlton Forbes and Pat Oakden, an opening bowler of real promise, whose career was soon to be cut short at the age of only 23 by a ruptured Achilles tendon.

Batting at no. 5 after Tom Dollery had won the toss, I soon found myself at the wicket with the score at 28–3. Wickets continued to tumble at the other end until Tom Dollery, batting as he always did at no. 11, joined me and we proceeded to share a last-wicket stand of almost 100 before I was out: bowled by part-time leg-spinner Alan Gill for 89, having batted for 131 minutes and hit thirteen 4s.

Tom Dollery didn't say a word as we walked back to the pavilion; he didn't need to. I had thrown my chance of a maiden century in the 2nd XI Championship away and my only consolation was that Tiger Smith had not been there to witness my impetuous folly. But as I made my way back into the dressing room his words kept ringing inside my head: 'You're getting ahead of yourself, young man.'

Perhaps the reason my apprenticeship was seven years long was because I was a slow learner. My second innings against Nottinghamshire would certainly suggest that this was the case. Once again I did the hard work and found myself in that state of relaxed concentration where mind and body were working together in seemingly perfect harmony. My second 50 of the match came in eighty-eight minutes and the next 40 runs in less than half that time. It was only then, as I glanced up at the scoreboard and saw 90 next to my name, that the doubts started. My pick-up suddenly felt mechanical, my feet were heavy and my eyes strained in the light. Faced with a situation I had never encountered before, panic had set in and all those good intentions had evaporated.

'Don't get ahead of yourself.' 'Take guard and start again.' 'Only play the ball that's coming.'

It was all forgotten, however, when I was stranded for what seemed like an eternity on 98, and – desperate to retain the strike at the end of an over – I turned the ball onto the leg side and set off without looking. It was a carbon copy of the mistake I had made at Old Trafford on my 2nd XI Championship debut. The only difference was that on this occasion I was run out for 98 rather than a duck.

Yes: I had made progress, but nowhere near enough to satisfy my increasingly exacting standards. The only consolation was that my two innings in the match had made a significant contribution to our 129-run victory.

My run of good form did not go unnoticed, however, and just a few days later I was summoned to Leslie Deakins's office not only to be awarded my County 2nd XI cap, but also to be informed that I had been selected to make my debut for the 1st XI against Surrey at the Oval in the match beginning on 6 July.

3

Debut, Doubts and Determination

While the runs I had scored in the 2nd XI put me in contention for selection for Warwickshire's 1st XI, I was under no illusions about the main reason for my promotion. MJK Smith had been named in the England team to play South Africa at Trent Bridge. This meant that it was almost certain that I would have no more than two matches to make my mark before MJK's return to the county circuit.

Only a couple of seasons prior to 1960 it would have been a daunting prospect indeed for any young player to make their debut at the Oval. The mighty Surrey team of the 1950s had carried all before them, winning seven successive Championship titles between 1952 and 1958.

As so often happens in sport, however, the aura of apparent invincibility had gone. The Surrey bowling attack in particular had lost its potency after the retirement of Peter Loader and Jim Laker. Indeed, as I scanned the Surrey team sheet on the morning of the match, I took much comfort from the fact that, of the bowlers included in the opposition team, Alec and Eric Bedser were now both past 40 years of age, left-arm spinner Tony Lock had been struggling for wickets since the controversy over his action had forced him to remodel it, and seamer Tony Allom was making a debut that proved to be his first and last Championship match. Aside from the awkward angle and swing offered by the left-arm bowling of David Sydenham, there didn't seem much to fear, particularly as the Oval wicket had proved a batting paradise throughout the season.

Ossie Wheatley, who was our captain in the absence of MJK Smith, won the toss and elected to bat on a beautiful summer's day. It seemed a perfect day to be making my debut and as I walked back to the pavilion after pre-match practice I couldn't help but reflect on what Tiger Smith had said to me the previous day, just before I'd set out on the journey to London: 'When you get in, Dennis, stay in; don't throw it away; you can't score runs back in the dressing room.'

How right he was! For 109 overs during our first innings I sat stuck in the dressing room alongside the rest of the Warwickshire middle order: Alan Townsend, Ray Hitchcock, Barry Fletcher and John Kennedy. There we all were, champing at the bit, desperate to get into the action but denied the opportunity as our opening batsmen filled their boots and left ours empty. At the end of the day our score stood at 377–0 declared; Norman Horner 203 not out and Billy Ibadulla 170 not out. Needless to say, there was no second innings and thus I returned home still without a first-class run to my name.

If events at the Oval had left any doubts as to the obvious but painful truth of Tiger's words that 'you can't score runs unless you are out in the middle', the following match against Somerset at Edgbaston dispelled them. This time Norman Horner and Billy Ibadulla shared a much humbler opening stand, but their 174 partnership nevertheless ensured that, batting at no. 7, I was once again denied the opportunity to bat on a flat pitch against a pretty ordinary attack.

With MJK Smith due to return from England duty for the next county match I was obviously frustrated and upset that my chance to stake a claim to a more regular place in the 1st XI appeared to have gone by default. What's more, it seemed little consolation to be included in the 12 for the next Championship game against Nottinghamshire at the Courtauld Ground Coventry, as I would far rather have had the chance of a knock for the 2nd XI in their fixture against Worcestershire than carry the drinks in Coventry for three days.

On the morning of the match, however, MJK – who was nursing an injury he had developed during the Test match – declared himself unfit to play. Thus it was that I got another chance to prove myself. I felt like the condemned man in the 1931 film *The Front Page*, played by George E. Stone, who gets a reprieve seconds before the switch to the electric chair is due to be thrown.

Once again we won the toss and batted, and this time it was Ray Hitchcock, the gritty New Zealand left-hander, who delayed the moment when I first walked out to bat in first-class cricket. Applying himself with characteristic tenacity, he made his way to a painstaking century. On this occasion, however, wickets fell at the other end at regular intervals and with the score at 162–5 the moment finally arrived for me to show what I could do. As I stepped out of the pavilion on my way to the middle I remembered what Tiger had told me time and time again about adjusting to the conditions. 'Look up, not down, and remember to blink – get your eyes used to the light – get them focused – get them ready.'

Standing at square leg and halfway to the wicket was the imposing figure of umpire Ron Aspinall. 'Good luck, son,' he whispered as I passed him.

'They must all know it's my first innings,' I thought to myself and my heart missed a beat before racing momentarily as if to catch up with itself. More advice from Tiger sprang to mind. 'Deep breaths, always take deep breaths. Fill your lungs with air; get the oxygen flowing.'

Arriving at the crease, I tapped my bat behind my right foot before looking up to take my guard.

'Two please,' I said in a voice so hollow and reedy it was a wonder that Sid Buller heard me.

'That's two,' he replied, and I tapped the bat again to mark the spot he had indicated before looking up again to survey the field. It was at this moment that the fact that I was about to receive my first ball in first-class cricket really registered and my nerves began to jangle.

'Right arm over, three balls to go,' said Sid Buller, lowering his left arm as a sign to bowler John Springall that he could proceed. I gripped the bat tight and tapped it nervously once more behind me as the Notts medium-pacer began his 12-yard approach to the wicket.

'Head still; eyes level,' I said to myself as the bowler gathered himself into his delivery stride. 'Meet the ball with the full face of the bat, play straight.'

As John Springall's bowling arm came up and over, I moved in synchronised reflex to the release of the delivery, simultaneously transferring my weight to the front foot. Then with left elbow high, my head and eyes over the ball, I played a good-length ball pitched on off stump back up the pitch with a forward defensive stroke that was technically perfect.

No more than military-medium in pace, John Springall nonetheless had an excellent command of line and length and for two and a half overs I could do no more than I had done with that first delivery – meeting each successive dot ball with the full face of the bat.

An older and wiser Dennis Amiss would have taken all this in his stride; he would have drawn on more than twenty-five years of batting experience to put the situation in context. 'Don't worry, don't panic,' he would have said. 'Take your time; wait for the bad ball; it'll come; take a deep breath; calm down and be patient.'

Without the benefit of such wisdom and experience, however, I began to feel the pressure of not scoring grow as other less rational voices took over my thinking. 'For God's sake get on with it. You haven't got all day. You're supposed to be out here to score runs, not practise the forward defensive ad infinitum.'

After fourteen more perfectly directed deliveries John Sprinall finally erred in length and line, dropping one a little shorter and wider of the off stump. Back and across I struck it hard off the back foot into a gap to the left of mid-off. Instantly setting off, I failed to spot the figure of Mike Haynes swooping in from extra cover. In one almost seamless movement, he picked the ball up one-handed and threw it right over the top of the stumps into the gloves of Geoff Millman, who routinely removed the bails leaving me stranded 10 yards or more from the safety of the crease.

I was run out for a duck in my first County Championship innings, just as I had been two years before at Old Trafford on my 2nd XI debut, and I walked off the field feeling utterly deflated. Nevertheless, I still had the prospect of a second innings in which to salvage something from the wreckage and two days later I went in to bat again with our score on 133–5 having lost three quick wickets. It was a tense situation and I knew that a further collapse would give Nottinghamshire a great chance of victory.

Perhaps because my nerves had been exhausted and purged by the disappointment of the first innings, I felt calm and composed as I walked out to the wicket. The fact that Nottinghamshire's prolific wicket-taker, Bomber Wells, was operating from one end didn't faze me in any way and I proceeded to bat throughout the rest of the Warwickshire innings, enabling Ossie Wheatley to declare and leave Notts a competitive total.

My 36 not out may not have been a huge score, but I had the satisfaction of holding the side together at a critical moment. With this in mind, I wondered if I might have done enough to retain my place in the side for the next match against Worcestershire at Edgbaston. MJK would definitely be returning but Barry Fletcher was having a lean run of form and had failed twice in the match against Notts. There was always a chance that he would be dropped and I would keep my place.

The resolution to the selection of the side for the next match involved one of the most bizarre episodes of my career. As I had hoped, even though MJK was fit to return to captain the side I was named in the 12 for the derby game against our local rivals.

There was nothing exceptional about the pre-match routine; a brief warm-up was followed by net practice before MJK went out to do the toss with Worcestershire captain Don Kenyon, who made the right call and elected to bat. Just half an hour later I walked proudly out onto the Edgbaston turf as part of the Warwickshire side. Ossie Wheatley marked out his run-up and MJK started setting the field. Before he could tell me which position to take up, Jim Stewart interrupted proceedings. 'Skipper, I hate to point this out but we've got twelve men on the field.'

'So we have,' replied MJK as he did a quick head count. It was then that he turned to me. 'Dennis; you're not playing. You're twelfth man.'

'Thanks a lot, Skipper,' I replied. 'Somebody might have bothered to tell me.' And off I trudged, much to the amusement of one or two of the other senior players. Barry Fletcher, whom I passed at fine leg as I walked off the field, could barely look me in the eye. He must have known that it had been a close call between him and me, but to his great credit he made the best of his reprieve, scoring a hard-fought 75 not out in Warwickshire's first innings.

I wasn't selected for the first team again until the last four Championship matches of the season and I really couldn't complain about my exclusion. Apart from 62 against Shropshire in the Minor Counties competition, I didn't score enough runs to merit a recall. In fact, it was something of a surprise in mid-August when I was named in the team to play Yorkshire at Edgbaston; but with Warwickshire languishing in 15th place in the Championship table the selectors had decided to give a couple of the younger players the chance of an extended run in the side.

My performances were little more than satisfactory; I flattered to deceive against Yorkshire before falling caught and bowled to Mel Ryan for 30. I also scored a gritty 43 not out on a tricky Dover wicket against Kent. Statistics, however, although rarely the whole story, cannot be entirely ignored and at the end of the 1960 season I had scored 135 first-class runs in 7 matches at the lowly average of 22.50.

As the season drew to its close I was puzzled more than depressed by my failure to score the runs that Tiger and Tom Dollery seemed to believe I was capable of. In the match against Middlesex at Lord's, for example, I had an insight into what was possible when batting with MJK. He was already well on his way to a dashing century, in the course of which he passed 2,000 runs for the season. His ease, confidence and panache at the crease made me all too conscious that there was some ingredient in my batsmanship that was missing. Whatever it was, it was evident that MJK, together with a handful of such illustrious contemporaries as Colin Cowdrey, Peter May and Ken Barrington, had discovered it.

Realising that something was missing was one thing; working out precisely what it was and putting it right was to take another four seasons. During that time, as a number of other more senior players were not retained by the club, I realised how fortunate I was that the Warwickshire Cricket Committee was prepared to give me more time to develop. While time may have been on my side, professional sport is an unsentimental business and you can only survive on the basis of being a 'promising youngster' for a relatively short period of time. After that it is almost inevitable that a younger 'hopeful' will emerge and take your place in the selectors' plans for the future.

The pressure on me to score runs, however, was intensified in March 1961 during an accident sustained during a football tour to France. I had in fact joined Warwickshire in 1958 as an all-rounder, and while my left-arm seam bowling was undoubtedly the second string to my bow it had provided me with the psychological security of knowing that if I failed with the bat, I had at least a chance of redeeming myself with the ball.

With the new season just around the corner Warwickshire had advised me not to go on the tour, but I was a regular member of Olton Football Club 1st XI and we played to a good standard in the Worcestershire Combination League. Not only was the prospect of visiting Paris irresistible but I was also at an age when most young men and women believe they are invincible.

Going up to head a ball in a match played on a rock-hard pitch against one of the stronger Paris sides, I collided with my opposite number, who fell on top of me with the result that I seriously jarred my back. Barely able to walk on my return to England, I was referred to Mr Gissane, a spinal surgeon. 'I'm afraid you're going to need an operation to fuse the damaged vertebrae in your back,' he told me.

'What if I leave it,' I replied. 'Will it get better in time?'

'If you don't have the operation, you'll be crippled by the time you're 30,' he replied.

'And if I do – will I be all right to play cricket again?' I asked.

'I'd say that even with the operation you have no more than a fifty per cent chance of playing again.'

It was as if my world had come to an end. The prospect of never playing cricket again was devastating. Even so, the odds of the operation being successful were insufficient to encourage me to go through with it, and thus it was that I hardly ever bowled seriously again, and I began the 1961 season facing the reality that my safety net had gone and that my entire focus had to be on batting.

Although being unable to bowl undoubtedly intensified my desire to succeed as a batsman, it didn't unlock the secret ingredient of how to score runs consistently. Indeed, by the time the 1964 season came around I was in serious danger of becoming just another player who had failed to make the grade. By the end of that summer I had played just 37 first-class matches in the five years since my debut at the Oval. More disappointingly, I had scored only 1,220 runs at an average of 21.40. By contrast John Jameson, who had also made his debut in 1960, became an established member of the Championship side in 1964, scoring over 1,000 runs and winning his county cap. In addition, competition for places in the Warwickshire 1st XI had become even fiercer following England batsman Bob Barber's move from Lancashire in 1963, and as I looked over my shoulder there were younger promising batsmen like Neal Abberley and Brian Richardson coming up on the rails.

There had been moments prior to 1964 when I seemed to be making progress; there had been an impressive maiden 50 in 1962 against a strong Yorkshire attack at Bramall Lane and a fluent 58 versus Kent in 1963. In between, however, there had been far too many failures and too many occasions when I had made a start and then inexplicably thrown my wicket away. I was also aware that, at the age of 21, I was no longer the callow 17-year-old whose mistakes could simply be put down to inexperience.

The harsh reality of my situation was made very clear to me early on in the 1964 season during a 2nd XI Championship match against Surrey at the Lockheed Sports Club in Leamington Spa. I was dismissed in the first innings for a prolonged duck by future England colleague Geoff Arnold. After I had played and missed for the best part of twenty minutes, he finally nipped one back to knock my off stump clean out of the ground and bring an end to the agony.

At the end of the day's play Arthur McIntyre, the Surrey coach who was well known for his straight-talking bluntness, took me to one side and dropped a bombshell. 'You won't like what I'm going to say, Dennis,' he said, 'but your game has gone backwards since I last saw you play. You're not going to make the grade if you carry on the way you're going.'

After the initial shock of Arthur's damning assessment it slowly dawned on me that he was only saying what everyone else was almost certainly thinking but had been too polite to say to my face. What's more, if I looked at the evidence in the cold light of day there was no escaping the truth of his words. Two seasons before, in 1962, I had scored 628 runs in the 2nd XI Championship in at an average of 44. The following season in the same competition in a similar number of innings my average had gone down to 34 and at the halfway point in the 2nd XI in 1964 I was averaging a mere 30. Arthur McIntyre's brutally honest intervention had not come a moment too soon, and in actual fact proved to be a critical turning point in my development as a cricketer.

It wasn't that I needed to work harder at my game or that my ambition to succeed had in some way diminished – far from it. Ever since I'd joined the ground staff in order to get extra time batting in the middle I had been the first to volunteer to play mid-week matches for any local club that was a player short. This hadn't changed and I still sought every opportunity for practice in order to get my technique as near perfect as possible. I was also still totally committed to gym sessions and training as hard as ever. So whatever it was that was missing had nothing to do with my work ethic, nor indeed my technique.

It was six weeks after Arthur McIntyre had dropped his bombshell that the answer to the puzzle finally came to me. I had been included in the team to play against Oxford University at Edgbaston in a match beginning on 1 July. I had yet to make a single appearance in the County Championship that season, and in my only other first-class appearance of the season against Cambridge University I had scratched around in the first innings for an embarrassingly slow 22 before being pinned plumb lbw by Richard Hutton.

Thus it was that going out to open the batting against Oxford on 2 July 1964 felt like my last chance. If I didn't take advantage of the relatively inexperienced university bowlers somebody else would and I would take yet another backward step down the rungs of the Warwickshire selection ladder.

In actual fact, the Oxford attack was by no means a pushover. Opening bowler John Martin and the two spinners, Maurice Mannasseh and Andrew Barker, ended up taking well over 200 first-class wickets between them in their relatively short careers. Indeed, poor Brian Richardson, who was opening with me, soon discovered that John Martin was a lot quicker than he looked; playing late to a swinging yorker, he was comprehensively bowled for 4.

John Jameson, who earlier in the season had demolished Essex on his way to a blistering maiden first-class century, joined me at the wicket for a partnership that would be the first of countless joint batting ventures over the next decade or so. In our contrasting ways, we set about repairing the early damage. As ever, John, with his bulky frame and muscular forearms, took the attack to the opposition, battering them into submission with fearsome power, never afraid to hit the ball in the air and over the field. My approach was more classical: looking to play straight with the full face of the bat, to time rather than strike the ball, to eliminate the possibility of getting out caught by keeping the ball on the ground. In boxing terms, if John Jameson was Rocky Marciano, always looking for the knockout punch, I saw myself as Sugar Ray Robinson, seeking to win the contest through style and grace as opposed to power.

After 5 overs of watchful defence my feet had begun to move automatically in concert with the bowler's arm; with each delivery, my head and eyes were in line with the ball at its point of release, my bat came up high and straight behind me and my body stayed sideways on to the oncoming ball. The movement into each shot felt equally natural, fluent and unpremeditated.

My first boundary came in the sixth over when John Martin, straying in length, drew me instinctively forward such that my bat came down on a half-volley length on off stump directly underneath my eyes. With an easy, flowing full extension of my arms I drove the ball off the sweet spot of the bat, with perfect timing, straight back up the pitch and past the bowler as he followed through, turning his head to see it accelerate over the rope in front of the pavilion.

I was up and away and batting with a poise and confidence I'd never known before at this level. I went past 20 with a delicate late cut off left-arm spinner Barker and got to 40 with an on drive for 4 off Manasseh. It was at this point that the home truths delivered to me just a few weeks before by Arthur McIntyre began to bear fruit. 'Don't throw it away, Dennis,' I said to myself under my breath. 'Forties won't do any more. Now you're in, make sure you fill your boots.'

Thereafter, in between deliveries, as I went past 50 and on into the 60s, I kept repeating the same message until, as I approached the 90s, I wasn't saying it any more because I didn't need to; I was 'thinking it' without having to remind or prompt myself.

At the end of 93 overs John Jameson and I had shared a second-wicket partnership of 255 and as I walked back to the pavilion with 114 to my name – my maiden first-class hundred – I knew that something funda-mental had changed during the course of that innings. Perhaps it had all been a matter of confidence, and scoring that first century gave me the all-important self-belief that had been lacking up to that point. Perhaps it was that I now had an insight into how to build and pace an innings at this level, as opposed to producing a cameo that was little more than a series of shots without real structure or foundation. Perhaps it was a combination of all these and other factors, including discovering a new level of concentration.

Whatever had changed, I am in no doubt that Arthur McIntyre had been the catalyst. His frank observations had forced me to look long and hard at myself and I hadn't liked what I'd seen. The truth is that, through a combination of a lack of opportunity and failure to take my chances when they came, I had found myself stuck in a catch-22 of county

2nd XI cricket. I was trying to develop my game for the demands of first-class cricket by playing at a lower level.

It wasn't that anything had been fundamentally missing from my batsmanship. Indeed, I had, in the words of Eric Morecambe, 'been playing all the right notes but not necessarily in the right order'. The Arthur McIntyre encounter had shaken me up; it had given me a new sense of urgency and a recognition that I had to take control of events before they took control of me.

It had taken me 31 matches to score my first first-class century. Hypothetically speaking, had I continued at that rate, bearing in mind that counties then played 32 matches per season, it would have taken me until 2064 to score my 100th century, by which time I would have been aged 121. Bearing in mind, however, that from 1960 to 1964 I was only selected for an average of 8 matches per year, it would in actual fact have taken me it more than four times longer than that, which would have meant reaching the great landmark just shy of my 500th birthday!

4

Committed, Capped and Courting

As the 1964 season ended I knew that my future progress in the game depended on playing regular first-class cricket. I was also well aware that this was by no means guaranteed at Warwickshire, so when Gloucestershire let it be known that they wanted to sign either me or my teammate Terry Riley in order to strengthen their batting resources, I was sorely tempted to drive down to Bristol and persuade John Mortimore, the newly appointed captain, that I was the man they were looking for.

While it is a regular occurence in today's game, moving counties was still unusual in the 1960s. It wasn't a prospect that I relished, not least because Warwickshire was the county of my birth and Edgbaston my 'Theatre of Dreams'. What's more, all my closest friends were linked in some way or other to the club or Birmingham and so I decided to bide my time. My plan was to seek reassurance as to my future at Warwickshire before taking things further.

The opportunity presented itself when the playing staff assembled for winter nets in preparation for the 1965 season. The urgency of discussing my situation with the captain or chairman of the Cricket Committee had intensified because of the news that Norman Horner and Ray Hitchcock, stalwarts of Warwickshire's batting line-up since the early 1950s, had decided to retire. It seemed to me that if I didn't feature in the club's plans for the future now I never would and that it would be time to move on.

As luck would have it, at the end of our first winter net session I found myself in the showers with the club captain, MJK Smith. 'Do you mind if I ask you something, Skipper,' I began.

'Of course, not,' he replied. 'What do you want to know?'

'Gloucestershire have shown an interest in signing me, but now that Norman and Ray have retired and there are a couple of batting places up for grabs here I'm wondering what to do and whether I should stay or go.'

'Suit yourself,' he replied as he picked up his towel and started drying himself.

It was hardly the positive affirmation I had been hoping for, and what rankled was the knowledge that had John Jameson asked the same question, MJK's response would have been totally different. John was the kind of player the skipper really liked: a potential match winner who, for all his inconsistency, possessed the rare ability to destroy an attack and turn the entire course of a game in no time at all.

As it turned out, however, MJK's non-committal response to my enquiry did not precipitate my departure to Gloucestershire. Quite the reverse, in fact; it fired my determination to dig in and prove myself to the skipper and anyone else who might have had any doubts about my ability.

'I'll show you,' I said to myself as I made my way home that night. 'You wait and see.'

The truth, of course, is that I was saying it more to myself than an imaginary MJK or anyone else but, whoever my muttering was intended for, there was no way I was going to give up, and thus it was that Terry Riley made his way to Gloucestershire while I stayed at Edgbaston to fight my corner.

The season began well. I was selected for the first match against Scotland, scoring a fluent 68 batting at no. 6. I soon followed this up with a run of good scores in the County Championship including 86 in my only innings of the match against Glamorgan at Newport and two more scores of 86 and 72 against Somerset. Further half-centuries over the next six weeks against Sussex, Yorkshire and Notts ensured that by the end of June I was an established first team player.

This was officially confirmed by the club on 9 July at Edgbaston when I was awarded my county cap during the match against Gloucestershire. Although still only 22, and comparatively young by cricketing standards, the seven-year apprenticeship that I had undertaken to get to this point made me feel older than my years but, nonetheless, immensely proud of the achievement.

This was the affirmation that I had been looking for during my exchange with MJK, but whether or not he had meant to use reverse psychology, his non-committal response in the winter had been every bit as motivating as Arthur McIntyre's blunt intervention the previous year. What's more, it made the moment that MJK handed me my county cap all the sweeter. 'Congratulations, Dennis,' he said, 'it's well deserved.'

Coming from MJK it was praise indeed. He was a man for whom actions spoke far louder than words and to that extent his style of captaincy suited me down to the ground. Just as I had always responded so positively to Tiger Smith's directness and honesty, I found MJK's quietly understated approach to leadership motivating. Perhaps because I respected him so much as a player, I wanted above all to prove myself to him. A nod of approval or a quietly muttered 'well played' meant more to me coming from the skipper than some of the outpourings of effusive praise that emanated from less informed sources.

As so often happens in sport, however, the celebrations that followed the award of my cap were relatively short-lived. While the first half of the season had begun with a bang, the second half ended with a comparative whimper. After three successive half-centuries in mid-June I didn't get past 50 again until the return fixture against Somerset at the end of July, and apart from a battling 55 against Essex my highest score throughout the entire month of August was a rather dismal 36 not out.

In horse-racing terms, I had faded in the final furlong. Nevertheless, by the end of the summer I could reflect on the fact that I had passed the milestone of 1,000 runs in a season for the first time. On the other hand, although I felt that I now belonged at this level, there was no escaping the reality that my tally of 1,423 runs had been compiled in

53 innings at the unspectacular average of 28, nor that after a total of 69 first-class matches spanning 6 seasons I had still only one century to my name.

Perhaps the most pleasing aspect of the 1965 season was the improvement in Warwickshire's overall performance. While finishing 11th in the County Championship was not a cause for popping the champagne corks, there was marked progress from the previous summer when we had languished towards the bottom of the table in 15th place. What's more, the emergence of a group of younger players including John Jameson, David Brown, Neal Abberley and myself gave supporters real hope that the best was yet to come.

The 1965/66 winter was to prove a real turning point in my development – and not just as a cricketer. Having spent the previous seven years working in the family tyre business from late September through to the end of March, I jumped at the chance of taking up a coaching job at Kimberley High School in South Africa's Northern Cape. I knew nothing about the repressive system of apartheid that denied the majority black, Asian and coloured population any say in the governance of South Africa and to be honest, even if I had been well versed in the politics of the country, I would still have gone.

The anti-apartheid movement that came to prominence in the UK in 1970 under Peter Hain's leadership had not as yet emerged as an effective pressure group, and South Africa was still very much part of the international sporting fold when I boarded the *Union Castle* in late September 1965 for the 8,300-mile sea voyage to Cape Town. Also on the ship were a host of other English professional cricketers including John Snow from Sussex, Derek Taylor and Fred Rumsey from Somerset and Jackie Bond from Lancashire.

For someone who had never been further than Paris on a four-day football tour, the next six months were a real eye-opener. I saw for myself the dehumanising impact of a system that classified people as second-class citizens in their own country, and I was horrified by the glaring inequality in the standard of schools, hospitals and housing provided for the white and black communities.

The unavoidable issue was whether my work as a coach at a highly privileged all-white boys' school was in fact supporting apartheid. It was mainly because of this that I jumped at the chance to assist with the coaching of children from schools designated for black children. This proved to be a really rewarding experience which strongly influenced my view that the people who would suffer most if international sportsmen and women stopped going to South Africa would be members of the already disadvantaged black, Asian and coloured communities. Rightly or wrongly, it was this view that largely determined my decision to return to South Africa the following winter and, some years later, to accept an invitation to participate in the highly controversial 1982 'rebel tour'.

Living for six months in such a different environment undoubtedly broadened my horizons on life. It was the first time that I had been without an established social network of family and friends to support me, and I soon discovered that, if I were to make the best of my time away, I would have to take the initiative to meet new people and visit new places. It was a challenge that I relished and by the time I got on the plane to fly home I had travelled the length and breadth of the country visiting game reserves, historical sites, cultural centres and museums, areas of outstanding natural beauty and lots of wonderful beaches. Moreover, I had established a new network of friends and developed a spirit of independence and a level of self-confidence I had never known before.

The icing on the cake was the quality of the cricket that I had played every weekend for Kimberley High School Old Boys in the regional league premier division. Matches were two innings per side and were split over two successive Saturdays. The wickets we played on were not only excellent for batting but they had the pace and even bounce of the best English pitches and were thus an ideal preparation for the coming summer at Edgbaston. What's more, the cricket was of a remarkably high standard and genuinely competitive.

There were only eight teams in the region's top division and they included all the players who were fighting for a place in the Griqualand West provincial side that competed in South Africa's Currie Cup competition; selection was entirely dependent on performances in the premier division club matches. This meant that every Saturday the opposition included current or aspiring members of the state side who were out to prove themselves.

I soon realised that with only one opportunity to bat each week it would be a crime of unspeakable proportions to throw my wicket away, and by the end of the South African season I had become the anchor of the Kimberley High School Old Boys' batting side. I also discovered that occupation of the crease intensified my passion for batting and sharpened my determination to bat on even longer. Indeed, I think that the seeds of the double-centuries that I went on to score in Tests against the West Indies have their roots both in Tiger Smith's advice that 'once you get to a hundred take guard again and go and get another' and also in that South African summer when I was desperate to make every one of those few innings count.

By the time March 1966 came around I couldn't wait to get home, not because I hadn't had a wonderful experience in South Africa, nor simply because I was looking forward to the challenges a new season with Warwickshire might bring. Just twelve months previously I had been invited for a night out at the Imp Cellar Club in Bromsgrove by my Warwickshire teammate Brian Richardson. The plan was for me to make up a foursome; Brian's girlfriend of the time, Sal Ouston, had also invited a friend of hers whom, she believed, needed cheering up following a recent split with a long-term boyfriend.

This was my first meeting with the charming, witty and beautiful Jill Evans and I knew immediately that I wanted to see her again. After a few dates, however, we had gone our separate ways, almost certainly because I was too wrapped up in myself and my cricket to leave space for anything or anybody else. But coming away to South Africa had given me the time and space to reflect on what really mattered to me, and whenever I found myself away from cricket and alone with my thoughts, it was Jill who was uppermost in my mind.

I think now that 'growing up' would be the best way of describing what had happened to me in the twelve months between March 1965 and April 1966. Stepping out of my comfort zone by going to South Africa, and meeting the woman with whom I wanted to spend the rest of my life, had widened my perspective and opened me up to the heretical possibility that there could be much more to life than just scoring runs.

The irony was that as my horizons broadened, my batting improved beyond all recognition. Having batted at no. 6 throughout the previous summer, I found myself promoted to no. 3 for the first match against Leicestershire at Nuneaton and, after failing in the first innings, I went to the wicket with the score at 27–1 with the strict instructions to take the attack to Leicestershire. The challenge was to post a decent declaration target while allowing enough time to bowl the Foxes out. Just ninety minutes later I was bowled by Terry Spencer for a rapid-fire 79 that had swung the momentum of the match our way.

Our 39-run victory was the perfect way to start a new season and in addition to my innings there were runs from Neal Abberley, Billy Ibadulla, MJK and John Jameson. What's more, the batsmen had been backed up by some genuinely hostile bowling from David Brown. A comprehensive victory over Essex in the second match indicated that our young Warwickshire side was going to be a force to be reckoned with in the Championship.

It was an exciting time and I relished the additional responsibility of batting at no. 3. While nerves had often got the better of me in the past, I now seemed to thrive on the adrenalin that came with challenging moments of pressure. In the match against Middlesex at Lord's, for example, I held our first innings together on a green pitch with uneven bounce. As wickets tumbled around me it was clear that avoiding a heavy defeat was entirely down to me, and with grim determination I grappled my way to an ugly but deeply satisfying 66.

In the first eight Championship matches of the season I went past 50 no fewer than seven times but was nonetheless frustrated that I didn't seem to be able to go on to that all-important target of three figures. 'Don't let it prey on your mind,' I kept saying to myself. 'Don't let it get to you.' But no matter how often I tried to reassure myself that it was only a matter of time before I cracked it, my failure to convert 50s into 100s was a matter of concern.

The breakthrough finally came at Edgbaston towards the end of May, and it proved to be a cause for double celebration; not only did I reach three figures for just the second time in my first-class career, but I also passed the career milestone of 3,000 runs. All I wanted to do now, however, was keep on batting and, having raised my bat to acknowledge the crowd's appreciation, I did exactly as Tiger Smith had always advised. 'When you get to a hundred take a fresh guard and start again.'

When we finally declared on 401–4 I had scored an undefeated 150. Even so, I was not entirely satisfied. Yes, I had scored a big hundred, and yes it was a first-class match, but my first century had been against Oxford University and now my second was against Scotland. 'Do they really count?' I asked myself. 'I need to prove myself against the best. I need to get a hundred in the Championship against one of the top sides.'

Getting out two games later for 97 against Gloucestershire on a flat pitch at Ashley Down, Bristol, didn't help. What made matters worse was that I had unaccountably missed a perfectly innocuous straight ball from Tony Brown.

'Where am I going wrong?' I said to Tiger on my return to Edgbaston.

'You're not,' he replied. 'But if you carry on fretting about this, or anything else for that matter, you'll make it go wrong.'

This was by no means the first or the last time in my career when I risked allowing a perceived rather than a real problem to erode my confidence. Fifteen years later when playing in the World Series in Australia I experienced a long run of low scores which led to me experimenting with my grip, my stance and balance at the crease. I was batting with Eddie Barlow for the WSC World XI against the WSC West Indies XI and I felt particularly out of sorts. At the end of an over when I had struggled to hit the ball anywhere near the middle of the bat, I went up to Eddie at the non-striker's end to ask for his advice.

'I don't know what to do, Eddie. I feel so uncomfortable at the crease. I don't know whether to stand with my feet wider apart or closer together or try going back to standing sideways on to the bowler.'

'Forget all that nonsense. You're not watching the ball from the bowler's hand,' he replied.

Of course Eddie was right. My tinkering and self-examination had become obsessive and introspective to the point where I was ignoring the fundamentals of the game. I was similarly in danger of losing all sense of proportion in my early days at Warwickshire because of this frustrating inability to turn promising starts into the really big scores that distinguish the stars from the journeymen.

In spite of this tendency towards irrational anxieties the 1966 season continued to go well for the team and me personally. Convincing wins over Somerset and Glamorgan ensured that we were lying 5th in the Championship table at the halfway mark in the season. Then, towards the end of July, my consistency was rewarded with selection for MCC against the 1966 West Indies touring side at Lord's.

Since my retirement as a player in 1987, I have been asked on countless occasions why I was so successful against the West Indies in my Test match career but failed so spectacularly against Australian sides even when they had far less threatening attacks. I have always maintained that the foundations of my success against Holding, Roberts, Garner and co. stemmed from the confidence gained during my first encounter against the West Indians in 1966.

I acquitted myself well for MCC at Lord's, scoring 69 and 47 against a bowling attack including Wes Hall, Lance Gibbs and, of course, the great Garry Sobers. Just a fortnight later, however, I did even better in Warwickshire's fixture against the tourists at Edgbaston. Although we were totally outclassed as a side and lost in the end by a margin of 10 wickets, I batted in the second innings with a focus and tenacity that I had never known before. Opening with Billy Ibadulla, I batted throughout the Warwickshire innings for 117 overs finishing on 160 not out.

As I walked off the field at Edgbaston to rapturous applause I felt as if a huge weight had been lifted from my shoulders. I had proved at long last that I was capable of making big scores against the top sides.

I have a strong suspicion that the freedom with which I hit the ball that day was influenced by my experience of batting in the relatively new one-day competition. Introduced in 1963, the Gillette Cup was the first official one-day trophy competed for by all the first-class counties together with a few of the leading Minor County sides. Perhaps because in those early days one-day cricket was regarded as something of a novelty that was not to be mistaken for the real game, there seemed less pressure, particularly on batsmen. Getting out playing shots could be forgiven as an inevitable consequence of playing with the attacking spirit demanded by the one-day game.

Although I had only played five matches in the Gillette Cup prior to 1966, I had already found the ethos and atmosphere of this new form of cricket very much to my liking and my one-day batting average of 40 included a match-winning 53 not out against a Lancashire bowling attack led by Brian Statham, Ken Higgs and Peter Lever.

Our first-round Gillette Cup match of 1966 was played against Glamorgan at St Helens Ground, Swansea, and I still vividly remember the excitement I felt on the morning of the game. It was exactly the same exuberant feeling that every school pupil experiences when breaking up for the summer holidays. 'This is going to be fun,' I thought to myself.

And it was fun! We batted first and I went in at 40–1 and promptly hit the first two deliveries from England fast bowler Jeff Jones for sizzling boundaries – the first off the front foot through extra cover and the second, a square cut off the back foot, past Tony Cordle's despairing dive. My century came up in 115 minutes and included fifteen 4s and a 6, but the highlight for me wasn't the hundred, nor the fact that we won the match by 165 runs; what pleased me most was the 126-run partnership that I had shared with MJK Smith. What's more, in the time it took MJK to get 48 of those runs, my contribution had been 78!

Subsequent victories over Gloucestershire and Somerset in which I scored 62 and 80 not out respectively secured our place in the final at Lord's against Worcestershire on Saturday, 3 September. With a side that included players of the quality of Basil D'Oliveira, Don Kenyon, Len Coldwell, Jack Flavell and Norman Gifford, our opponents were the clear favourites. What's more, Worcestershire arrived at Lord's at the end of a successful season during which they had been narrowly pipped by Yorkshire for the County Championship title.

At the end of a memorable day out at Lord's, however, it was the thousands of Warwickshire supporters who had made the journey to London who were able to cheer as MJK Smith lifted the Gillette Cup. In the morning they had witnessed Tom Cartwright produce an almost unplayable spell of classic English seam bowling which resulted in the astonishing analysis of 3–16 off 12 overs including 4 maidens.

The ball continued to seam around throughout the day, but when it came to our innings Bob Barber and I dug in, scoring 66 and 44 respectively as we laid the foundation to overhaul Worcestershire's modest total of 155 with 5 wickets in hand.

With the Gillette Cup Final marking the end of the season we were able to look back on a summer in which we had won the county's first trophy of any kind for twelve seasons. We had also made real progress in the Championship, finishing in a highly respectable 5th position. My contribution to the campaign had been 1,663 runs in first-class matches at an average of just under 40. In the Gillette competition my tally of 299 runs in four innings gave me an average of almost 100.

There was, however, one other key event that I had the coming winter to reflect on. England had fared disastrously against the mighty West Indies throughout the 1966 summer, losing three of the first four Test matches by wide margins. Thus it was that, following my 160 not out against the tourists for Warwickshire, I was summoned to the Oval as part of a major team overhaul to play my first Test match for England.

5

First Test, Failure and Fulfilment

Of the eleven England players who had taken the field for England in the disastrous Fourth Test at Headingley, five were dropped for the final match of the series at the Oval, including Colin Cowdrey. He was replaced as captain by Brian Close, who had been in the international wilderness since the previous West Indies tour in 1963. Also recalled were John Edrich, Ray Illingworth and John Murray, who was replacing Jim Parks as wicketkeeper.

Unusually, the England selectors only named eleven players for the match, and so I knew before I arrived at the Oval for team practice the day before the game was due to start that I would be making my Test match debut for England. Whether the certainty of playing is an advantage or not is debatable but as a debutant I felt the weight of expectation grow heavier in the countdown towards the day of the match.

In actual fact, I have little recollection of the details of that practice day. Doubtless, I took my turn batting in the nets, but if my timing and foot movement were in good order or not I have no idea. It all flashed by in a state of nervous apprehension that was heightened by the realisation that everyone else in the side had been in this situation before. 'They know what to expect,' I thought to myself. 'They all know each other; they've all played together before, been on tour together. I'm the odd one out.'

As the day continued my insecurity grew into a sense of neurotic unease that I really didn't belong in such company and that I was there under false pretences. 'How can my name appear on the same team sheet as Tom Graveney, Geoff Boycott or Bob Barber?'

It never occured to me, of course, that even though they'd played for England before, some of the others were almost certainly feeling as apprehensive as me about the five days ahead of them. John Edrich, John Murray and Ray Illingworth, for example, would have been every bit as anxious to justify their recall as I was to prove my worth in my first Test.

The point is that, in stark contrast to the modern game, there was at that time little or no awareness of sports psychology in professional cricket. The culture of the game was such that no one dreamed of articulating their anxieties for fear of being thought weak and unmanly, and so, like everyone else, I worried in silence while putting on a brave face and pretending that all was well.

In the midst of all this emotional turmoil, however, there is one moment of that practice day that I remember vividly. It was when Brian Close presented me with my England cap and sweater, each bearing the crown and three lions that I had first marvelled at as a boy when I watched Denis Compton walk out to bat against the 1953 Australians. My pride was such that I slept in my new England sweater the night before the match.

As was customary in those days, on the evening before the Test there was a dinner attended jointly by the players and the selectors. It was a formal occasion and, after the final course had been eaten and cleared away, Doug Insole, the chairman of selectors, delivered a speech full of the usual 'backs to the wall' platitudes: 'This is our chance to turn back the tide; to salvage our national pride; to snatch victory from the jaws of defeat; to rise like a Phoenix from the ashes … etc., etc., etc.' On completion of his version of Henry V's address before the Battle of Agincourt, he and all the other selectors departed, leaving Brian Close to brief us on how he wanted the match to be played. He started by taking us through the West Indies' batting line-up one by one, pointing out their strengths and weaknesses, and instructing the bowlers on how he wanted them to attack each one.

When he came to Garry Sobers he turned to John Snow. 'Right, Snowy,' he said, 'when Garry comes to the wicket – the first ball you bowl at him – I want it to be the fastest bouncer you can muster.'

There was a pregnant pause before Snowy gave his considered response. 'You've seen the wicket, Skipper. It's going to be as flat as a pancake – no pace – no bounce – and Garry's the best hooker in the world, for God's sake. If I bounce him the ball will disappear into the playground at Archbishop Tennyson's Grammar School.'

'I don't care what you think,' replied a defiant Brian Close. 'You do what you're bloody well told and let me worry about where the ball ends up!'

As it happened, Bob Barber and Basil D'Oliveira were bowling when Sobers came to the wicket in the West Indies' first innings and so John Snow was unable to put the skipper's plan into operation. In their second innings, however, David Holford was run out going for a quick single off Snowy, bringing Garry Sobers to the wicket with three more balls of the over remaining.

Brian Close, in typical fashion, immediately planted himself at bat-pad, inches from the West Indian captain as he took guard. Having given a cursory glance around the field, Sobers then settled himself down before John Snow began his characteristically rhythmical approach to the wicket. Following the skipper's instructions to the letter, he leaped into his delivery stride, prematurely dropping his left shoulder in order to dig the ball into the middle of the pitch with every ounce of energy he possessed.

While the ball may have left Snowy's hand at upwards of 90 miles per hour, it rose off the benign Oval pitch in a gently curving parabola at no more than medium pace. In a flash Sobers was into position for the hook shot with a bat-lift so high he could have struck the ball over the famous Oval gasholders. His rapid movement in preparation for the shot was followed by an equally swift full swing of the bat – too swift, in fact. The ball arrived long after the shot had been played and, ballooning off

Sobers' left glove, it dropped straight into Brian Close's hands at bat-pad. Off trudged the great man, out first ball, caught Close, bowled Snow, for nought.

'There you are, Snowy,' said Brian Close as he walked up the pitch to greet the fast bowler, 'it all worked out exactly as I said it would.'

There's no doubt that after a summer in which the England side had been totally demoralised, Brian Close's absolute self-belief and supreme competitiveness were precisely what was needed.

His bloody-minded refusal to accept the validity of any view other than his own provided a clarity of purpose that didn't allow for wavering or weakness of any kind. Even when Bob Barber badly damaged his finger during the match, Brian refused to accept that he was unable to bowl. In his mind, Bob's leg-spin was critical to his plans and thus, in spite of his complaint that he could hardly hold the ball, the skipper made him bowl 37 overs in the match. The fact that Bob took 5 critical wickets including Sobers in the first innings was proof enough to Brian that he had been right. In his mind the end had justified the means.

As far as my own performance in my debut Test was concerned, I might have done better with a little more of the skipper's blinkered self-belief. As it was, the exceptional form that had won me selection for the Oval Test deserted me from the moment that John Edrich was caught behind off Garry Sobers with our first innings score on 85–3 in reply to the West Indies total of 268 all out.

As I picked up my bat and made my way to the dressing-room door, already putting on my batting gloves, I was no more than subliminally aware of the voices of my teammates.

'All the best, Dennis.'

'Get stuck in, mate.'

It's when you first close the dressing-room door behind you at the beginning of your journey out to the wicket that you realise, as a batsman, that you are on your own. And as I made my way out of the Oval pavilion and down the steps towards the outfield, I had never felt so lonely or isolated in spite of a crowd of around 20,000 people.

Almost as soon as I stepped onto the outfield I had to pass the daunting frame of Wes Hall, who was fielding at fine leg. 'Good luck, young man,' he said, and smiled without a hint of irony.

With my mouth so dry and tight from the nervous tension of waiting to bat, I walked by unable to reply or return the smile. It was then that my instinct kicked in and I began to go through my established routine: adjusting my eyes to the sunlight, practising a forward defence shot, followed by a drive, and then – one, two, three, four short running steps to get my feet moving. As I neared the middle, Tom Graveney, the not out batsman, joined me for a brief word of encouragement: 'Just watch out for the one Sobers swings back into you; otherwise there's not much movement. Good luck! You'll be fine.'

But something was telling me I wouldn't be fine and somehow I felt out of sorts; my bat felt heavier than usual and I ached somewhere – a tired kind of an ache – but I wasn't exactly sure where it was coming from.

It was only three days since I had scored 160 not out against pretty much the same attack, but it might as well have been three decades as I played and missed at the third ball I receive from Garry Sobers. 'Get your feet moving,' I said to myself, and the next ball they moved back instead of forward and I was late down on a full-length ball that oh-so-nearly got past my hideous defensive prod.

It's no consolation that at the other end Tom Graveney was batting with sublime grace and poise. As he eased his way towards a chanceless 165 not out I cannot have been the only person at the Oval that day to wonder how on earth such a great player could have been overlooked by the England selectors for more than three seasons.

Tom Graveney's wonderful innings laid the foundation for our eventual victory by an innings and 34 runs. It was a remarkable achievement and I was proud to be part of an England team that had dramatically reversed the summer's cricketing fortunes. Nevertheless, I couldn't escape the disappointment of my own personal contribution.

My batting had been so entirely without authority or rhythm that it was a mystery how I had hung on long enough to amass my meagre total of 17. It must have been a relief for the packed Oval crowd when Wes Hall produced a lightning-fast delivery of full length. Neither forward nor back, the ball thudded into my pads which were the only obstacle preventing it from knocking my middle stump out of the ground. Umpire Charlie Elliott's gnarled forefinger shot up in instant response to the West Indies' rapturous appeal and off I trudged back to the pavilion, on a walk that seemed to take twice as long as it had on the way out just forty-three minutes earlier.

My failure was all the more poignant when looked at in comparison to the contributions made by the other players who had been brought in for the match. John Murray had shared a partnership of 217 with Tom Graveney before being dismissed for 112; John Edrich, batting at no. 3, had steadied the ship along with Bob Barber after the early loss of Geoff Boycott; Ray Illingworth bowled with accuracy and guile to take 4 economical wickets and Brian Close led from the front with towering authority. Sadly, I was the glaring exception to the adage that 'the new broom always sweeps clean'.

It didn't take me long to realise that it was the pressure of the occasion and not a lack of ability that had undone me. This was finally confirmed in my mind just two weeks later when Warwickshire played the West Indies for the second time in the season at Edgbaston. This time the match was a 50-over one-day contest.

Although we fell marginally short of the tourists' total of 257, I almost saw us home with a run-a-ball 76 which included twelve 4s and a huge 6 over long-on off Lance Gibbs. Thus it was, that in the four matches I had played against the West Indies that summer my overall tally was 398 runs at an average of 79.

'I can do it. I know I can,' I kept saying to myself as I relived that Test debut in my mind time and time again over the course of the next few weeks. 'And the next time I'm selected for an England side I'm damn well going to prove that I'm good enough to be there.'

I didn't have long to wait. Two weeks after the season had ended a letter arrived from Lord's informing me of my selection for the MCC under-25 tour of Pakistan; to be regarded among the best players of my generation was a real boost to my confidence. England had no Test series during the winter of 1966/67, so the MCC squad was a strong one: captained by Mike Brearley, with my Warwickshire chum David Brown as vice-captain, the party also included Alan Knott, Derek Underwood, Geoff Arnold, Pat Pocock and Keith Fletcher, who were to form the nucleus of the future England team.

The tour proved to be a challenging two months, not least because MCC's budget for the tour was Scrooge-like in its meanness. Our accommodation was basic in the extreme, and on arrival at our hotel in the remote town of Sahiwal, close to the Afghanistan border, we found goats in our bedrooms. What's more, there was only one shower, which had to be shared by the entire team during our week-long stay.

It was a genuine culture shock and, given the stifling heat, the isolated locations and the 'Delhi belly' that affected almost all of us during the trip, it could have been a thoroughly miserable experience. In fact the reverse was true, and we quickly became a cohesive and tight-knit group. This was partly because concerns about security severely restricted our opportunities to explore and socialise beyond the confines of our accommodation. More significant, though, was the relaxed and purposeful culture that was fostered by Les Ames, the manager, and skipper Mike Brearley.

It was evident from the outset that both men had a deep mutual respect, and there was no doubt that the gracious and thoughtful example that they provided was central to the happiness of the tour as a whole. At team meetings our personal contributions were actively encouraged such that we felt a shared responsibility for the success of the trip. In addition the manager and skipper treated us as individuals, recognising and celebrating our differences. At one extreme we had the extrovert ebullience of the ever-cheerful Robin Hobbs and at the other there was the sardonic dryness of Richard Hutton's Yorkshire wit. Both had me in stitches on numerous occasions and helped us all to take our minds off the oppressive heat or our troubled digestive systems.

We also enjoyed excellent leadership on the field and Mike Brearley's subsequent success as England captain came as no surprise to those of us who had played under him in Pakistan. Tactically astute, he was particularly adept at selecting which bowling combinations would work best for different batsmen or at particular stages in the match. His use of the unfailingly accurate Derek Underwood in tandem with Robin Hobbs's flighted wrist-spin was a case in point; Robin was able to attack with confidence from one end knowing that, even if he went for the odd boundary, Derek would pin them right back the following over.

The quality of Mike's analytical mind was well illustrated by his post-tour prediction that Pakistan's lack of fast bowlers, their batting difficulties against pace bowling on fast pitches, and their lack of a settled pair of opening batsmen, would all present problems for them on their forthcoming tour of England. He proved correct: Pakistan lost the 1967 Test series in England 2–0 for all the reasons he had predicted.

The highlights of the MCC under-25 tour's tightly packed itinerary were undoubtedly the three four-day 'Test' matches that were scheduled against the Pakistan under-25s. Similar to our team, they included cricketers like Asif Iqbal, Mushtaq Mohammed, Wasim Bari and Majid Khan who were destined to be the mainstays of their senior national side for the next decade or more.

The flat, mud-baked wickets that we played on throughout the tour were excellent for batting even though they became more receptive to spin as matches progressed. The real issue, though, was maintaining concentration and avoiding dehydration in the intense, acrid heat of a Pakistan summer.

By the time of the first 'Test' at the Bagh-e-Jinnah ground in Lahore, however, we had acclimatised well and won our two warm-up matches against the South Zone and the Central Zone with relative ease. I had batted particularly well against a strong South Zone attack, scoring 47 and 75 in the match, and I was delighted not only to be included in the final eleven for the first 'Test' but also to be given the responsibility of batting at no. 3.

It is almost impossible to overstate the physical and mental demands of playing cricket on the subcontinent; for 154 overs lasting well into the second day we fielded in a temperature never falling below 40°C as the Pakistan batsmen made their way to 429–6 declared. Mushtaq Mohammed and Majid Khan both batted with supreme authority on their way to chanceless centuries.

In reply we were soon 8–1 when Mike Brearley was caught behind playing an understandably tired shot to Majid Khan's rather gentle off-spin. Having spent most of the previous two nights awake listening to cockroaches scuttle across my hotel bedroom floor, I too felt tired as I made my way to the middle. 'Mind over matter,' I said to myself. 'You've got to make this count.'

Once I'd got used to the blinding glare of the Lahore sun and the fact that the ball was already beginning to turn, I began to find my way. Two consecutive cover-driven 4s off left-arm spinner Salahuddin, followed by a well-timed late cut to the boundary off leg-spinner Mushtaq, stimulated my adrenalin, and suddenly I was no longer conscious of the weariness I'd experienced as I'd walked out to bat.

The real pleasure of that innings, however, came from the partnership that I built with Keith Fletcher. For the best part of five hours we batted on together, overcoming the various pressures of the occasion: spin bowling of the highest quality, oppressive heat and growing weariness. If one of us showed signs that the flame of concentration was fading, the other came down the wicket to reignite the fire. We encouraged each other, gave praise to shots well played and reassurance when the ball beat the bat.

Perhaps it was a case of the 'nervous 90s', or simply a matter of exhaustion from having batted for 320 minutes, but on 99 I played a limp, half-hearted drive at Salahuddin, offering a simple chance to the substitute fielder at mid-off. By contrast, Keith Fletcher went on to a richly deserved hundred.

It was Les Ames who helped me overcome the disappointment of getting out one run short of a century. 'Well played, Dennis,' he said. 'You gave a fine display of technique and temperament out there today. I was impressed.'

'Thank you, Manager.'

'A word of advice if you don't mind – next time you go to the wicket just remember that building a big innings is not dissimilar from driving a car on a long journey; you have to start in first gear, change up smoothly to second as the revs increase, then go into third, then fourth and you only go up into overdrive when you've got that hundred behind you, and even then you still keep within the overall speed limit.'

Every word he said made total sense and, because the man talking to me about how to play a long innings had himself scored 102 first-class hundreds, his observations had real authority and significance. The fact that I scored successive centuries in the next two matches is indicative of the impact Les Ames's advice had on me.

An authoritative 102 against the President's XI in Rawalpindi was followed by 131 in the Second 'Test' played in Dacca a fortnight later. It was in this innings that I batted longer than I had ever done before, occupying the crease for 450 minutes during a partnership of 356 with Mike Brearley. Although I was very much the junior partner in contributing little more than a third of the runs we added together, I played the anchor role which enabled a dominant Mike to take the attack to the opposition.

While there was frustration at the end of the three-match 'Test' series that all the games had ended in a draw, in spite of us enjoying some commanding positions, nearly all of us returned to the UK with enhanced reputations. For my part I had contributed 284 runs in the three 'Tests' at an average of 94.66. What mattered more than the statistics, however, was that I had become close friends with a significant number of my teammates.

In many ways, though, the highlight of the tour was meeting and getting to know Les Ames. One of the undisputed greats in the long history of the game, he was nonetheless by instinct a moderniser and one of the earliest advocates of the introduction of the one-day game into the cricketing calendar. Moreover, his belief in youth, which made him the perfect choice as manager of the under-25 squad, was clearly evident in what he was doing as secretary/manager of Kent County Cricket Club. He had been responsible for overseeing the development of young players of the calibre of Alan Knott, Derek Underwood and Bob Woolmer.

What I didn't know on that tour, of course, was just how closely my life and career would parallel his. It wasn't just that at the end of our playing days Les and I would have both scored 102 first-class centuries, nor that we would have played an almost identical number of Test matches, albeit thirty years apart. What we also came to share was a lifetime's involvement in cricket; just as he followed his playing days as a cricket administrator, becoming secretary/manager of his beloved Kent, so I took a similar path in taking up my role as chief executive of Warwickshire.

We also both experienced up close the fierce backlash that comes with cricketing controversy; Les had to deal with the stigma of being a member of the infamous 1932/33 'Bodyline Tour' to Australia, while nearly fifty years later I had to contend with the hostile reaction to World Series Cricket and the rebel tour to South Africa. What's more, I'm sure that for both of us it was these crises and the entrenched reaction of the establishment that helped shape our shared view that, if the game is to survive, it must continue to evolve and modernise to keep pace with the changing times.

At the end of those two months away in Pakistan I came back to the UK a more mature and complete batsman than I had been before the trip. In addition, a seed of understanding about the nature of leadership had been planted somewhere inside me. This was not to come to full fruition for more than twenty years but I have no doubt that I have Les Ames to thank for its eventual harvesting.

6

Resilience, Recall and Rejection

If anyone wanted to do a research project on the central significance of confidence to sporting success, I would strongly advise them to include a case study of my career from the beginning of the summer of 1967 through to June 1972.

Returning to England on the 'high' of my performances during the MCC under-25 tour of Pakistan, I enjoyed a highly productive summer in 1967 averaging well over 50 in first-class cricket for the first time in a season. What's more, I scored five centuries including 176 not out against Nottinghamshire, 161 not out against Northamptonshire and 151 against Leicestershire.

It seemed that I had finally unravelled the mystery of how to follow Tiger Smith's advice on reaching three figures: 'to start again and get another hundred'. What's more, I felt there had been a fundamental change in my mindset before going out to bat, such that the earnest hope of scoring runs had been replaced by confident expectation.

It wasn't that I had developed a greater motivation or ambition to succeed, nor that I had in some way become suddenly more tenacious. The difference was that throughout the 1967 County Championship campaign I was wholly undistracted by doubt and went to the wicket innings after innings in that state of relaxed concentration that enables the mind and body to move in harmonious concert.

I was in the form of my life and under any normal circumstances I would have seen my selection for the Second Test against India as a wonderful opportunity to establish myself in the England batting line-up alongside Tom Graveney, Ken Barrington and John Edrich. In reality, though, I knew that my tenure in the side was likely to be short-lived. Indeed, the only reason that I was included in the 12 for Lord's following England's convincing 6-wicket defeat of India in the First Test at Headingley was that the selectors had controversially decided to drop Geoff Boycott for slow scoring. He had batted for the best part of ten hours in making 246 not out.

Boycott fans (including, of course, Geoff himself) accused the England selectors of hypocrisy in dropping him for slow scoring while retaining Ken Barrington, whose 93 had been equally painstaking.

There was no doubt in my view that Geoff's 246 had laid the foundation for England's eventual victory and that there are often circumstances in Test cricket when maintaining a fast scoring rate is of secondary importance to building as large a first-innings total as possible.

Whatever the rights and wrongs of the decision to drop Geoff Boycott, however, everyone knew that having made their point the selectors would recall him in the not-too-distant future. What's more, with all the England batsmen in the runs, I knew in my heart of hearts that I would be the one to make way for his return.

Not surprisingly, when I arrived at Lord's on 22 June for the first day of the match against India, my mindset was completely different from just a few days before when I had driven in through the gates of the County Ground, Northampton. On that occasion I had no doubt not only that I would be playing against Northants that day but also that, as long as I didn't get injured, I would be occupying the no. 3 berth in the Warwickshire side for the rest of the season.

The confidence and certainty that come with a feeling of belonging cannot be seen or measured but are as fundamental in making a cricketer feel secure as all the protection equipment that we wear as a safeguard against injury.

These days we are beginning to recognise the significance of mental health and take action in support of the psychological and emotional well-being of players. In 1967, however, any attempt to alleviate the stresses and strains of playing competitive professional sport was regarded as molly-coddling.

Obviously, players face very different issues depending on their status in the game. As someone who was on the fringes of England selection for the first three or four years of my Test career, I feel sure that the affirmation and security of the central contract system that was finally introduced in 1999 would have made a world of difference to me and many others who had similarly taken their time to establish themselves at Test level.

The point is that we are not all blessed with Ian Botham's confidence. His unshakeable self-belief was such that he burst onto the Test arena as an instant success with 5-wicket hauls and rapid-fire centuries. Mike Gatting, by contrast, was something of a cricketing yo-yo: in and out of the England side, playing thirty matches over seven years, before finally scoring the first of his ten Test centuries against India. What's more, it took the hugely talented Andrew Flintoff twelve matches spread thinly over four years before he got to three figures in Test-match cricket. Even more remarkably, given his subsequent success, 'Freddie' didn't record his first 5-wicket haul in an innings until his 33rd Test match for England.

Although I came into the side for the Second Test against India on what was undoubtedly a temporary basis, I certainly didn't disgrace myself. In the first innings at Lord's I played fluently, sharing in a solid second-wicket stand with Ken Barrington, before being bowled for 29 by a beauty from one of India's great spin triumvirate, Bhagwath Chandrasekhar.

As in my first Test the previous summer, I was now treated to a batting masterclass by Tom Graveney. In a chanceless innings of 151 he began by nullifying the threat that the Indian spin triumvirate of Bedi, Chandrasekhar and Prasanna posed on a wicket of slightly uneven bounce. Making his way smoothly up the gears, assured defence gave way to graceful attack before the power of his driving forced six Indian fielders back onto the boundary as he scored freely and at will against the greatest slow bowling attack in the world.

We duly won the match by an innings and 24 runs and so I was denied the opportunity of a second chance to make my mark. With media pressure growing for Boycott to be recalled to the side, I had little doubt that I would be discarded for the Third Test. The selectors had other ideas, however, and it was poor John Edrich who made way for the jubilant Geoff Boycott.

While I was delighted to be retained, particularly as the match was at Edgbaston, I could not help but feel sorry for John Edrich. The decision to drop him was the perfect illustration of what an unsentimental business selection is. Only a couple of seasons previously John had played brilliantly for England in both home and away series against Australia, scoring characteristically gritty centuries at Lord's and Melbourne. Moreover, just six months after being dropped for the Third Test versus India he would be scoring 96 at Sabina Park, Kingston, followed by 146 at Bridgetown, Barbados, during England's successful series in the West Indies. Such are the vagaries of form and fate, but meanwhile, however, John's bad luck was my good fortune.

Aside from the nervous excitement and anticipation that I felt at representing England in front of my home crowd in Birmingham, I was, along with every cricket lover in the country, curious to see Geoff Boycott's response to his recall.

It quickly became apparent to everyone in the England dressing room that if the aim of the selectors' disciplinary action had been to encourage Geoff to become a more engaged and committed member of the team they had failed miserably. For a man whose entire waking life had been devoted to the pursuit of scoring runs, punishment for scoring a Test double-century must have been incomprehensible. The fact that the rebuke had been so public had only added insult to injury with the result that, if anything, Geoff became even more withdrawn, isolated and self-contained than before.

If Geoff Boycott had written the script for the Edgbaston Test against India he would, of course, have played the starring role, scoring undefeated centuries in both innings. Alas, although we won the match by the substantial margin of 132 runs, the plot did not work out as he would have wished. Indeed, he found himself cast in a distinctly minor role, scoring just 25 and 6. His only consolation was that the selectors could not possibly have complained about his second innings as his 6 runs were scored in two minutes off just 5 balls!

My contribution to the match came in the second innings when, with our score at 34–3, on a turning wicket, I shared in partnerships with Tom Graveney and Brian Close before being caught for 45 off a ball from Prasanna that bounced and turned. I was, of course, disappointed not to reach what would have been my first half-century in Test cricket, but I had the satisfaction of having played a significant role in ensuring that we could set the kind of target that would give us a good chance of victory.

As the second-highest scorer in England's critical second innings I felt that I had done more than enough to be retained in the side for the First Test against Pakistan that was due to be played at Lord's just two weeks later. As a consequence, my omission in favour of Basil D'Oliveira was a huge disappointment, particularly as no explanation was given by either the captain or the selectors. The sense of injustice that I felt was only intensified when I scored a fluent half-century for Warwickshire against Pakistan at Edgbaston five days before the Test match was scheduled to start.

The truth of the matter was that I had been given a taste of Test cricket and found the added spice very much to my liking. By comparison the flavour of county cricket now seemed just a little bland and under-seasoned. Nevertheless, I knew full well that unless I maintained my hunger for runs at county level there would be no chance of dining again at the top table of international competition.

Successive scores against Leicester, Scotland and Yorkshire were sufficient to bring me a recall for the Third Test at the Oval. With England ahead in the series and the prospect of a winter tour to the West Indies beckoning, the selectors were clearly exploring who to take to the Caribbean as the extra batsman. With Boycott, Cowdrey, Barrington and Graveney absolute certainties and Jim Parks firm favourite to tour as the wicketkeeper/batsman there were only three more batting berths up for grabs.

I knew that Basil D'Oliveira was a strong candidate for selection, not just because of his skill against the short-pitched ball, but also because he had an uncanny ability to break partnerships with his deceptively gentle medium-pace bowling. In addition, some of the more influential cricket correspondents were pressing John Edrich's claims. Jim Swanton, writing in the *Telegraph*, said that 'not only has Edrich got an enviable record against bowling of genuine pace but, as a left-handed batsman, he has the potential to disrupt the West Indian bowlers' line of attack'.

The general consensus was that the only matter of debate for the selectors was whether to take Colin Milburn or me. Both of us were young and would benefit from touring experience even if we didn't end up playing in any of the Test matches. We also both had excellent records against the 1966 West Indies side. My main advantage was that I was considerably fitter than the 18-stone Northamptonshire opener; the case for selecting Colin was that he had made his runs against the West Indies in Test matches, whereas my big scores against them had been for MCC and Warwickshire.

Amazing though it may seem, there was no real protocol back in the 1960s for informing players if they had been selected for international duty or not. Thus, the fact that I had heard nothing prior to the day of the announcement of the touring party did not necessarily mean that I would not be included, and so, like everyone else in the country who was interested, at 2.30 p.m. on Friday, 22 September 1967, I turned on the radio to discover my fate.

I was bitterly disappointed to be the one who missed out on what proved to be a triumphant tour of the Caribbean. Selection for an International XI to tour India and Pakistan in February and March came as no consolation as all the old insecurities began to surface and nagging doubts ran through my mind. 'Am I good enough to play Test cricket?' 'How can I become a better player?' 'Where am I going wrong?' I could easily have slipped into a winter-long depression but for a key event that has changed my life for the better in every way.

On Saturday, 28 October 1967, Miss Jill Evans officially became Mrs Jill Amiss on the occasion of our wedding at St George's church,

Edgbaston. It was a glorious autumnal afternoon and as we came out of the church after the ceremony, we were greeted by a cricketing guard of honour. My brother Alan and Jim Evans (my new brother-in-law), together with Warwickshire cricketers David Brown, Neal Abberley, John Jameson, Roger Edmonds, Terry Riley and best man Bryan Richardson, all with bats raised aloft, formed an archway under which Jill and I walked hand in hand as husband and wife.

With all the excitement of the honeymoon that followed in Tenerife and the excitement of moving into our new home on West Drive, just a Jos Buttler T20 shot from the Edgbaston ground, there was little or no time to dwell on thoughts of cricket. Indeed, as the departure date for the International XI tour of Pakistan and India loomed, for the first time in my life, the prospect of playing cricket did not seem that appealing.

As it happened, though, the short tour of the subcontinent proved a real adventure. Our manager was Joe Lister, the secretary of Yorkshire County Cricket Club, and Micky Stewart captained a side that also included future England captains Mike Denness and Tony Greig, along with Keith Fletcher, Derek Underwood, Geoff Arnold, Jack Birkenshaw and Roger Tolchard, all of whom, of course, were destined to play Test cricket.

Our tour began in Pakistan with the first match against the Pakistan Control Board President's XI in Karachi, and we were soon embroiled in a controversy that almost caused a diplomatic incident. It was a four-day match and by the end of the third day the wicket was beginning to deteriorate such that there were areas where the surface was crumbling badly. With the Pakistan side due to bat last, the state of the pitch was very much to our advantage.

The following morning when we arrived, however, all the gaps and cracks had been filled with clay. Joe Lister, never a man to mince his words, lodged an official complaint and told the Pakistan authorities that unless the pitch was returned to its original condition we would not continue with the match. After much debate involving telephone calls to and from respective cricket and government authorities, the newly laid clay was removed from the wicket and the match resumed with our spinners, Jack Birkenshaw and Gamini Goonesena, bowling us to a 43-run victory.

The tour was a success from both a team and a personal point of view. My second innings runs in our victory in Karachi were followed by a chanceless hundred which helped set up an emphatic win over an Indian XI in Bombay and a rapid-fire half-century against a strong Chief Minister's XI in Madras.

Our achievements on the subcontinent, however, were of little consequence as far as the media were concerned. The success of Colin Cowdrey's side in the West Indies and the prospect of the arrival of Bill Lawry's Australian touring party dominated the cricketing headlines as the 1968 domestic season got under way.

Having been in such good form throughout February and March, I couldn't wait to get started. Stories were circulating that following some late-night incidents on the Caribbean tour disciplinary action had been taken against Colin Milburn. As a result of this there was much speculation that he would be out of the selectorial pecking order for the foreseeable future.

I liked Colin Milburn immensely and recognised, along with many others, that he was the most exciting attacking batsman in the country. On the other hand, sport is a highly competitive affair and if Colin's indiscretions had given me a better chance of playing for England I was not going to complain or shed any tears. With the First Test against Australia scheduled to begin on 6 June, I had five weeks to make my case for selection.

As the London Weather Centre records, however, 'all of April and the opening 3 weeks of May 1968 were cool and unsettled with showers and prolonged spells of rainfall that were significantly above the average for the time of year'. The impact on the domestic cricket season was dire. Only 49 overs were bowled over the entire three days of our opening match against Sussex, and the following game versus Hampshire was similarly rained off with less than 50 overs played. Our next match against Essex at Edgbaston was restricted to one innings because of thunderstorms and, although I scored a half-century, the constant breaks for rain did not allow me to build up any sense of momentum.

When the clouds cleared in the last week of May I finally had the opportunity I was looking for in the match against Nottinghamshire at Trent Bridge. Having failed in the first innings, I went to the wicket with the score at 4–1 in our second dig, knowing that we needed to bat for four sessions to save the game. 'This is your big chance, Dennis,' I thought to myself as I walked out to the wicket. 'Don't mess it up.'

Having taken guard and flicked the last ball of Mike Taylor's over off my hips for a single, I got ready to face Carlton Forbes, Nottinghamshire's Jamaican-born seamer who was just a bit quicker than he looked. From previous experience I knew the key was not to get caught on the crease. 'Get your feet moving, Dennis,' I said under my breath. 'Look to get right forward – don't go halfway.'

In spite of all my good intentions, the frustration of sitting watching the rain pour down various pavilion windows for more than a month had got to me. Carlton Forbes's first ball thudded into my pads without me having moved so much as an inch out of the crease and up in the scorebox Peter Pike, the Warwickshire scorer, duly recorded the event: DL Amiss lbw b Forbes 1.

It was one of those moments when I half-wished our other batsmen would get out for low scores as well so that my own abject failure would seem less prominent. As it was, though, I spent the next day and a half witnessing a batting masterclass given by Rohan Kanhai. Having been dropped twice in the gully on just 10 by poor Ian Moore off Garry Sobers, he went on to score a quite brilliant 253, sharing in a record-breaking third-wicket partnership of 402 with Billy Ibadulla, who remained undefeated on 147.

By the time the selectors gathered at Lord's to pick the side for the First Test at Old Trafford against Australia, I had only passed 50 twice in six weeks. As someone whose form and confidence have always been inextricably linked to time spent at the crease, I was a little apprehensive at my inclusion as one of seven batsmen in the England 12. I didn't lose too much sleep, however, as I was pretty confident that I would be the one to miss out on the final cut. As it happened, though, when we arrived at the ground and saw mottled patches on the Old Trafford wicket the decision was made to play an extra batsman, and so I was listed in the side to bat at no. 5.

Australia won the toss and, in spite of doubts about how the pitch would behave, they elected to bat. In the first hour John Snow and Ken Higgs moved the ball at sharp angles off the seam with both Redpath and Cowper falling cheaply. At 29–2 the Aussies looked vulnerable. Bill Lawry and Doug Walters then came together, however, and battled their way to a 150-run partnership before falling in successive overs to Bob Barber's leg-spin.

This brought Paul Sheehan and Ian Chappell to the wicket, and showing typical Aussie grit, they slowly but surely wrested the initiative away from us, such that the Australian first innings ended on 357, well above par given the challenging conditions.

Our innings started well with John Edrich and Geoff Boycott seeing off the opening attack of Graham McKenzie and Neil Hawke with a solid opening partnership. From 86–1, however, we were soon 87–2, and then 89–3, with John Edrich, Geoff Boycott and Tom Graveney all gone in quick succession. Thus it was that with the Old Trafford clock registering 2.39 p.m. on an overcast Manchester afternoon, I made my way down the pavilion steps and began the walk out to the wicket to face the last ball of Bob Cowper's over.

Captain Colin Cowdrey greeted me in the middle and wished me good luck before I took guard. I then looked around the field before settling into my stance and playing a good-length ball from the Australian off-spinner back up the wicket without any difficulty.

With Colin Cowdrey taking a single off the first ball of the next over, I now found myself looking up the wicket at fast bowler Graham McKenzie, known as Garth because the intimidating strength of his highly developed physique matched a comic book character with the same name. With a run-up of no more than fourteen paces, he generated his considerable pace and bounce from the power and elasticity of his final delivery stride. Perfectly sideways on and with his shoulders and arms drawing back for the moment of release as an archer does the string of a bow, Garth had the ability to shape the ball away towards the slips in almost all conditions and this particular day was no exception.

Although I survived the remaining five balls of that over, I played and missed at three of them and as the Australian fielders changed positions in readiness for Bob Cowper to bowl the next over Colin Cowdrey came down the wicket to have a word with me. 'I always find that if I'm having a problem getting in line with the ball, it helps if I take my right foot back and across towards the off stump.'

'Thanks for the advice, Skipper,' I replied. 'I'll give it a try next over.'

Here was a man who was not only my captain and one of England's best post-war batsmen, good enough to have scored countless hundreds against some of the best bowlers to have played the game, but he was also playing in his 97th Test match. Who was I to ignore his advice?

In the next over from Graham McKenzie, just as he was about to release the ball, I duly took my right foot back and across towards the off stump as per instructions. The ball hit the seam, nicking the outside edge of my bat on its way into the safe and secure hands of first slip. As I walked back to the pavilion I couldn't help but visualise how it would read in the following morning's papers: 'DL Amiss c Cowper b McKenzie 0.'

The batsmen following me didn't fare that much better and we were bowled out all too quickly for a paltry 165. Australia batted again to set us a target of 412 on a wicket of uneven bounce and considerable turn. We knew we were up against it and after a steady start, wickets were soon falling again; at 91–3 I made my way out to the wicket for the second time in the match to face Bob Cowper.

Even before I took guard the psychological siege had begun. I was entirely hemmed in by a tight encampment of fielders: wicketkeeper, first slip, gully, short leg, leg slip, short extra cover – each of them within touching distance – crouching as if ready to pounce, all chewing gum, all with their eyes coldly fixed on mine.

The fact that I knew exactly what they were trying to do to me was irrelevant. The insecurities that surfaced after my first-innings failure had come out to bat with me once again, and so, in truth, it was my own self-doubt that got the better of me rather than any pressure the Australians could apply. Thus it was that after nine deliveries I played all around a perfectly innocuous ball from Bob Cowper and was on my way back to the pavilion without scoring for the second time in the match.

I was, of course, neither the first nor the last batsman to bag a pair so early on in my Test career. Graham Gooch was to go one better than me in 1975 when he was dismissed twice for a duck in his debut Test at Edgbaston, also against Australia. The challenge, though, is to overcome the psychological impact of what feels, at the time, like public humiliation.

As history records, I rebuilt my international career after the disaster of Old Trafford and went on to play 50 Tests, ending up with a batting average only marginally lower than Geoff Boycott's, but my miserable start against Australia left an indelible mark. In fact, I have often been asked how a batsman whose record against the West Indies, Pakistan, New Zealand and India was as good as the best of his generation could fail so spectacularly and consistently over the years against Australia. The answer, of course, is that I was never able to overcome the psychological advantage that the Aussies established over me during that match in 1968.

7

Confidence, Catharsis and County Champions

Although my confidence was in short supply for a long time after the disappointment of Manchester, there was no shortage of advice or comment from cricketing acquaintances: 'At least you've played for England, Dennis; that's more than most of us achieve'; 'You've got the cap, sweater and blazer with the crown and three lions on, mate; they can't take that away from you.'

Well meaning though most of these comments were, they were of no consolation. I had no desire to be one of the countless cricketers who play a couple of Test matches without making the grade before fading back into the obscurity of county cricket. If anything, my ambition to succeed was now heightened rather than diminished, not least because I felt a strong need to prove all those who doubted my ability wrong, particularly the told-you-so cricket pundits who delight in displaying retrospective wisdom: 'I knew he wasn't good enough; they shouldn't have picked him in the first place'; 'He won't make a Test-class batsman as long as he's got a hole where the sun doesn't shine!'

Whether or not the England selectors shared these sentiments I don't know, but it was to be three years before they felt that I had done enough to be selected again and during that time, in spite of my bloody-minded determination to make myself a better batsman, I seemed to go backwards before beginning to advance again.

Having been dropped from the Test side following my 'pair' at Old Trafford, I returned to county cricket where, no matter how hard I tried, I couldn't find any kind of form. In fact, it wasn't until 3 August that I put any kind of score together, making back-to-back centuries against Worcestershire and Kent. The fact that I returned to some kind of temporary form against these two particular counties may not have been entirely coincidental given that I had an especially good record against both sides. In the matches I played throughout my career against Worcestershire I actually scored 11 centuries. I also enjoyed considerable success in my twenty-seven encounters with Kent. In fact, one of my best-ever hundreds was on a raging turner at Gravesend with Derek Underwood in his pomp, threatening to run through us.

The point is that, from a batsman's point of view, playing against specific sides or particular bowlers or on grounds where you have previously made big scores can give you that slight psychological edge that ensures that it's your day and not your opponent's. It is, in effect, a reminder that if you have done it before you can do it again and keep on doing it. Put simply: 'success breeds success'.

Any boost in confidence that this end-of-summer flurry of runs might have given me did not change the fact that 1968 was a season I would have preferred to forget. With a first-class batting average of less than 30 there were legitimate concerns about whether I had a long-term future in county cricket, let alone playing again at Test level.

Any hopes that the winter break would clear my mind and that I would return for the 1969 season refreshed and reinvigorated were soon dispelled as I continued to struggle for form. In four successive early-season matches I struggled to 20s and 30s before giving my wicket away for no apparent reason, exactly as I'd done in the early days of my career.

My response was to spend hour after hour in the nets tinkering with my game, experimenting with a new grip or a slightly adjusted stance, in the vain search for a technical solution to what was, of course, a problem of self-belief and confidence. As a consequence my performances throughout the following summer of 1969 were only marginally better than the previous disastrous season, and there was no escaping the reality that my progress had not merely stalled but gone into reverse gear.

Although my star was in decline, the club's was undoubtedly rising. With off-spinner Lance Gibbs joining us in the second half of the 1969 season we were rapidly becoming a far more competitive outfit, winning seven matches to finish 4th in the County Championship table, as compared with 11th in 1968.

In spite of the team's progress, the personal frustration of being unable to find the touch and form that I knew I was capable of took its toll and by the end of the 1969 season I felt stale and tired. What I needed was some form of rehabilitation, and the offer of a six-month contract coaching at Selborne College, one of the leading schools in East London, South Africa, could not have come at a better time. I'd really enjoyed the six months in Kimberley a couple of years before this, and the prospect of getting as far away as possible from Edgbaston where everyone seemed to know my business was most appealing. Once I'd negotiated the provision of married accommodation so that Jill could accompany me, I signed on the dotted line.

Our destination was East London on the Indian Ocean in South Africa's Eastern Cape. The area is best known for its beaches and stunning scenery, and after we had spent a few weeks cooped up in a second-rate hotel in the city, Ray Johnson, a PE teacher at Selborne College, introduced us to Tony and Ann Wood, who offered us one of the holiday cabins they owned overlooking the banks of the magnificent Nahoon River.

We couldn't have had a more perfect location from which to explore the many places of extraordinary beauty in the Eastern Cape. These included the glorious headland and beach at Cove Rock, and the mystically meandering Buffalo River, whose source is hundreds of miles to the north in the Majuba Hills on the border between KwaZulu and Natal. The forested valley through which it flows on its way to join the ocean was full of rare species of insects, fauna and flora. We also spent time spellbound in the many game reserves as we watched elephants, lions, zebras and giraffes roam freely across a landscape that was as close to paradise as anything either Jill or I had ever seen before.

During the school holidays Tony and Ann Wood also took us to stay in a property that they owned in the Transkei, one of the most remote areas of the Eastern Province. If ever there was an opportunity to get away from it all then this was it. The roads were little more than dirt tracks and there was neither electricity nor running water in the area.

Jill and I had the time of lives enjoying the novelty of the experience, but we also recognised that while we could return to the luxuries and comforts of home, the Xhosa-speaking inhabitants of the Transkei had no such good fortune. Indeed, it made any problems that we had seem utterly trivial. All of a sudden, bagging a pair against Australia seemed nothing in comparison to the pain and suffering created by malnutrition, infant mortality and endemic diseases like malaria.

At the end of our six months in East London I couldn't help reflecting on how much both this trip and the time I had spent previously in Kimberley had broadened my outlook on the world and stimulated a desire to see and understand more. Perhaps this curiosity stemmed from being self-conscious about my limited academic and scholastic achievements. Whatever the reasons, I now recognise how important it is for the psychological health and mental well-being of professional sportsmen and women to engage in activities and interests outside of their sphere of competition.

Back in the late 1960s and 1970s players did not have the support of an influential organisation like the Professional Cricketers' Association that actively promotes and sponsors programmes to foster both the desire and the means for young players to prepare for a life beyond the narrow parameters of the game. The lack of such an organisation when I started my career perhaps explains why so many players of my generation found adapting to life after cricket so very challenging. In this context I count myself very fortunate. Apart from a relatively brief period when I worked outside cricket as a director of two companies, I am one of a privileged minority of players who have enjoyed the security of almost continuous employment within the game throughout their working lives.

The vast majority of professional cricketers, by contrast, find themselves by their early 30s, if not sooner, having to build a second career from scratch. Those who have not prepared themselves for this moment often lose their way, and there have been too many tragic cases of former cricketers ending up destitute and in despair. Brian Statham and Graham Dilley, two of England's finest post-war fast bowlers, are classic examples. Although from different cricketing generations, they both retired from the game utterly unprepared for life outside the game and lived out the last years of their lives in abject poverty and chronic ill health.

What my visits to South Africa helped me realise was the critical importance of striking the right balance. While I knew that success as a professional cricketer would not come without genuine focus and dedication, it was also becoming very clear to me that having nothing else but cricket in my life would be disastrous in the long run.

Meanwhile, during our stay in East London, I played for Selborne College Old Boys in the Eastern Province senior league and practised in the run-up to matches as hard as ever. I also went to the crease each Saturday with the same missionary zeal to score runs that I had always had. The difference was that between matches and practice sessions I was so absorbed in exploring new places, seeing new sights and meeting new people that I 'switched off' from cricket and all theories of batsmanship and discovered that I arrived for the next game more physically relaxed and mentally prepared than I had been for some time.

While Jill and I were sad to say farewell to South Africa and our many new-found friends, the long sea journey home on the SS *Windsor Castle* was every bit as relaxing and enjoyable as the six months we had spent in the Eastern Cape. Travelling with us were Mike Buss and Tony Greig and their wives, who were also on their way back to England for the new season. With fun and laughs aplenty, the highlight of the journey was our collective winning of the ship's fancy dress competition as Snow White and the Seven Dwarves. At 6ft 6in tall, but never afraid to lead from the front, Greigy made a surprisingly attractive Snow White.

I feel sure now that the significant improvement in my performances over the next two English summers stemmed in no small measure from the broadening of outlook that came with experiences like our trip to South Africa and the security and happiness that I was enjoying in my personal life. Throughout the 1970 season I scored runs far more consistently than in previous summers, such that continued good form in the first half of 1971 brought an England recall for the Test series against Pakistan.

I played in all three of the matches and scored my first Test 50 in the game at Lord's. In spite of this, a lack of consistency and my subsequent failure in the First Test against India meant that I suffered the indignity of being dropped yet again, knowing that no one else was to blame but myself. The selectors had given me four consecutive matches in which to stake a claim for a permanent place and I had blown it again.

Someone once said that 'fear is an inhibitor that has kept more people from fulfilling their destiny than any other one emotion,' and it may have been the recognition of this truth that helped me find a way to unlock the mental chains in which I was shackled every time I walked out to bat in Test cricket.

Meanwhile, however, with less than a month of the 1971 season to go, I had a bit more on my mind than looking for a way to make a breakthrough in Test cricket. Jill was due to give birth to our first child towards the end of August, and by the final Sunday of the month the baby had still not arrived. Perhaps unwisely, I set off early on the morning of the 29th to drive to Chelmsford for a John Player League 40-over match against Essex. I might as well have saved myself the journey, as no sooner had I arrived home late that night, miserable at having got a duck at Chelmsford, than I was back in the car. Jill was in considerable pain and I drove her to the hospital as fast as I could, anticipating that the birth would be imminent.

After a few hours of 'will she, won't she' indecision, reminiscent of Geoff Boycott's calling between the wickets, the midwife responsible for Jill's care told me to go home. 'Nothing's going to happen tonight, Mr Amiss,' she said. 'So you'd best go home and get some sleep.'

At 7 a.m. I was woken by a call from the hospital to tell me that Jill had given birth to a healthy 7lb 2oz baby girl, and while my absence did not greatly amuse Jill, it was the source of much good humour in the dressing room.

'Well, well, well, Dennis,' said one particular wag. 'What an amazing achievement! Within the space of twenty-four hours you've missed your daughter Becca's birth and David Acfield's armball!'

While Becca's arrival at the end of the 1971 season heralded significant changes in family life, the opening of the 1972 summer threatened to turn my cricketing career upside down.

Warwickshire had signed Alvin Kallicharan, which obviously intensified the pressure on places in the middle order, and because I was the batsman most out of form, with a highest score of just 17 in four innings in the opening two fixtures of the season, it was me who was surplus to requirements.

Having been in the England side just nine months before, this was a bitter pill to swallow. In fact, when AC Smith told me that I wasn't in the side for the opening County Championship match against Sussex, I gave serious thought to calling it a day at Warwickshire.

'Perhaps I should find another county,' I thought to myself as I came away from Edgbaston, 'or maybe I'm just not cut out for professional cricket; maybe I should just pack it all up and find an easier way to earn a living.'

It was yet another of those 'Arthur McIntyre' moments and the conclusion that I reached, following a long internal debate, is in many ways the best illustration of the stubbornness that David Brown has always accused me of: 'No way am I giving up,' I said to myself, 'not now – not after fourteen years of effort. I'm not going to throw that all away.'

And so it was 'back to the drawing board' of County 2nd XI cricket with a pig-headed determination that I would 'bloody well show them once and for all' what Dennis Leslie Amiss was made of. The first match was against Gloucestershire 2nd XI at Leamington Spa and because it was still early season, and their first team did not have a game, lining up against us was more or less their entire 1st XI, including David Allen and John Mortimore – two of the best off-spinners in the game.

'Just my luck!' I thought to myself as I walked out to bat on a wicket that was breaking up from virtually the first delivery of the innings. Realising that I had nothing much left to lose, however, I decided to throw caution to the wind and play my shots irrespective of the outcome, and as wickets tumbled at regular intervals around me, I took the attack to the Gloucestershire bowlers before being the last wicket to fall for 71 in a total of only 185.

It proved to be the highest score of the match on either side, by some margin, and this gave me considerable confidence going into the next game. It was against Leicestershire 2nd XI at Shirley and we were joined by John Jameson, who was playing following a run of bad form in the County Championship.

Having won the toss and elected to bat, I hardly had time to get my pads on before our first wicket fell. Making my way out to the middle, I passed a disconsolate John Jameson who was trudging back to the dressing room having been caught at slip for a duck.

Deciding once again on a policy of 'fortune favours the brave', I drove the first ball from Leicestershire seamer, Ken Spray, straight back past him for 4. Two deliveries later I repeated the shot before driving the next one through the covers, off the front foot, for another boundary.

I reached my century in just over a run a minute, but what pleased me most was the timing and the fluency of my strokeplay. While the bowling might not have been the most testing I'd ever faced, I knew that I was ready for the cut and thrust of the County Championship.

My recall duly came at the end of May against Essex at Chelmsford, but my delight at being back where I felt I belonged was tinged with disappointment when AC Smith informed me that I would be batting at no. 6. I knew, of course, that I simply had to accept it. With batsmen of the quality of MJK Smith, Rohan Kanhai and Alvin Kallicharan listed to go in above me in the middle order, I had no real grounds for complaint.

What I feared, of course, was that batting so low in the order would give me no time to build a substantial innings, and so it proved. I only had a handful of overs at the crease in the first innings before the declaration, and was stranded again in the second innings on 12 not out when the heavens opened and the last two sessions of the match were washed out.

The same pattern was more or less repeated in our next County Championship fixture at Worcester, and it was on the drive back to

Birmingham that I decided on a course of action that was to change the entire course of my career. With just four days before our next game against Middlesex I knew that there was no time to lose in implementing the plan.

The next morning I arrived at Edgbaston a good hour before net practice was due to begin and waited for AC Smith to arrive. I didn't have long to wait and the moment he arrived in the car park I was ready and waiting by the door of his car.

'I'd like a word, please, Skipper,' I said as he got out of the vehicle.

'Of course, what do you want to talk about?'

'I want to discuss my place in the team.'

'You'll be playing against Middlesex if that's what you want to know.'

'There's more to it than that, Skipper; I want the opportunity to make a real contribution to the team.'

'I'm sure you will, Dennis, and your chance will come.'

'No disrespect to you, Captain, but being realistic, if I carry on batting at number six, given the middle order we've got, my chances are going to be very limited.'

'What are you suggesting then, Dennis?'

'I want you to give me three matches opening the batting.'

'I'm not sure I can promise that.'

'Listen, Skipper, I've been looking back through the scorebook and, apart from two reasonably decent efforts against Northants and Worcester, our opening partnerships this season have been really disappointing. So what's to lose – I can't do any worse.'

The conversation ended with an agreement that I would open the batting against Middlesex in the next match. Beyond that AC was not prepared to make any firm commitment, but it was better than nothing. What's more, it allowed me to move on to the next stage of the plan.

For the next three days, when most of the team had gone home after official net practices, I persuaded Bob Willis and David Brown to bowl fast and short at me with new balls in the indoor cricket school. This was the preparation I felt I needed for doing battle with one of the best opening attacks in the country. Although very different in their styles,

Mike Selvey and John Price were highly effective operators, taking over 1,500 first-class wickets between them, and playing for England with distinction at different stages in their careers. While Mike Selvey was an ace exponent of seam and swing, John Price, on his day, was one of the quickest and most hostile fast bowlers in the country.

Just as I had hoped, David Brown and Bob Willis proved a fearsome prospect on the hard bouncy surface of Edgbaston's indoor school, particularly as the idea of helmets was still a long way off. As ball after ball whistled past my nose or thudded into my chest guard, I began to wonder whether putting myself in the firing line of opening the innings was such a good idea after all. Nevertheless, there was now no going back and as I persevered, little by little, I found my reactions sharpening as I started to sway out of the line of the short-pitched deliveries with increasing confidence.

On an overcast and humid Edgbaston morning in mid-June, Middlesex's Eric Russell and Mike Smith (not to be confused with MJK) came out to bat to face David Brown and Norman McVicker. The wicket was tinged with green and Norman in particular made excellent use of the new ball at his bustling fast-medium pace. Getting it to swing late and seam both ways, he had all the opposition batsmen in trouble. In Middlesex's lowly final total of 158 only Clive Radley made any significant contribution, battling away with grim determination for an ugly but hard-fought half-century as wickets tumbled around him.

It was mid-afternoon when John Jameson and I walked down the pavilion steps on our way to open Warwickshire's innings. The sun had come out and all the morning's green tinges seemed to have disappeared from the pitch.

'All we've got to do is see the new ball off,' said John as we approached the middle. 'Conditions are going to be perfect for batting this afternoon.'

He was absolutely right; after the initial bounce, zip and swing that the new ball almost always provides, the balance of the conditions tipped very much in favour of batting. Sadly for John, he was not at the wicket long enough to take advantage of this; hitting across the line of a straight ball from Keith Jones, he was adjudged lbw for not very many.

Rohan Kanhai soon followed him back to the pavilion and MJK Smith joined me in the middle. At the end of the day's play we were still together, having taken Warwickshire's total to 156 without further loss of wickets.

The following morning we carried on where we had left off, gradually asserting our dominance over the Middlesex attack before MJK was caught behind off the persevering Mike Selvey for 74 having shared in a 160-run partnership.

Alvin Kallicharan simply carried on where MJK had left off, making a run-a-minute half-century without seeming to break sweat. A master at working the ball off his legs and finding a gap in the field, Alvin rotated the strike almost at will, much to the annoyance of Fred Titmus, who had to change from bowling over to round the wicket at regular intervals.

After we had established a huge first-innings lead AC declared and, even as I walked off the field with 151 not out to my name, I felt that something fundamental had changed and that I was at the beginning of a new adventure – and so it proved; the following week against Worcestershire at Edgbaston I batted throughout our first innings for the second time in eight days to reach another undefeated 150.

'I think it's time to make this "opening the batting" arrangement permanent,' said AC as I sipped a cold beer in the dressing room at the end of the day's play. 'I don't know why but it seems to suit you.'

If there were any doubts about just how much opening the innings suited me they were allayed the following week against Lancashire. Batting with Rohan Kanhai, I shared in a stand of over 300, as I made my way to what was then a career-best 192. Then, in the following game against Kent at Dartford, I batted through our entire innings for the third time in as many weeks on my way to a match-winning undefeated century.

While the transformation that had taken place in such a short space of time appeared dramatic, the reasons for it were very clear. Having to sit, wait and watch others batting did not suit my temperament. Indeed, I can now see that the uncertainty of not knowing when I would be walking out to the middle had contributed to feelings of anxiety which had in turn undermined my self-confidence.

Paradoxically, perhaps, being given the additional responsibility and pressure of opening the innings bolstered my self-esteem. I felt not only that my new role was an indication that the skipper and selectors had faith in me, but also that I now had a central role in the side that afforded me the kind of status and responsibility I'd not had before.

From a psychological point of view, though, I believe that the most important thing of all was the way I had responded to disappointment and failure earlier in the season. While part of me wanted to duck away and hide from the humiliation of being dropped, there was another more powerful instinct to stand up and be counted. While it could, of course, have all gone horribly wrong, the experience of those few weeks was something that I was to draw on in future years, and, in particular, in my comeback against the West Indies in 1976.

Meanwhile, however, the 10-wicket victory that we had enjoyed over Middlesex at Edgbaston in June was the launch pad for what proved to be a Championship-winning season. Having last emerged victors in 1951, Warwickshire's success may have been long overdue but it was richly deserved as, throughout the season, we grew in collective confidence and played an irresistible brand of attacking cricket.

Undefeated throughout the entire summer, we would have enjoyed significantly more than the 9 victories we recorded in our 20 Championship matches but for the intervention of rain in several fixtures. Nevertheless, in the end we romped to the title by a clear 39-point margin over second-placed Kent.

The key to our success was not only that we all enjoyed each other's company on and off the field, but also that, as individual players, we were all committed to the team and to the mission of overturning nineteen years of underachievement and disappointment at Edgbaston.

The batsmen reigned supreme throughout the summer. Whether setting daunting first-innings totals in rapid time or chasing down fourth-innings targets against the clock, we were always up for the challenge with Rohan Kanhai leading from the front. Against seam or spin, on dry or wet wickets, whether setting a total or chasing victory, Rohan was always in control.

He was brilliantly supported in the middle order by MJK Smith who, at 39 years of age, was still a force to be reckoned with. His blistering hundred in our opening fixture against Essex not only set the tone for the season, but it was also a masterly demonstration of how to play spinners on a drying pitch.

Alvin Kallicharan, who batted at no. 5 to great effect throughout the summer, was never afraid to take the attack to the opposition. We were batting together against Worcestershire, for example, when Vanburn Holder was in the middle of a particularly hostile spell. At the end of an over during which the ball had whistled past my nose on more than one occasion, Alvin came up to me for a brief word: 'I think we need to see Vanburn off,' he said. 'He can't have too many more overs left in him.'

The next two deliveries he faced from his West Indian teammate were both hooked for enormous 6s. 'What on earth are you doing?' I called to him from the non-striker's end. 'I thought the plan was to see him off.'

'That's what I was doing,' he replied. 'It's just another way of doing it.'

In the bowling department, the main wicket-taker was Norman McVicker, whose nagging accuracy, nippy pace and ability to move the ball sharply in the right conditions brought him a handsome crop of wickets at an impressively economical rate.

Leading the attack were our fast bowlers, old hand David Brown and new boy Bob Willis. Bob had joined Warwickshire for the 1972 season, having been unable to establish a regular place in the Surrey side in spite of an England call-up for the Ashes tour of 1970/71. Surrey's loss, however, was our gain as his high arm, searing bounce and inward slant made him the perfect foil to David Brown, whose lower arm action tended to angle the ball away from the bat.

In support of the seamers, of course, we had one of the greatest off-spinners of all time in Lance Gibbs. A 'man for all seasons', he was capable of adjusting his pace, flight and line of attack dependent on the circumstances of the game or the surface. Thus, there were times during our Championship-winning season when he played the containing role with a level of economy that Scrooge would have been proud of. On other occasions, by contrast, he employed his bag of tricks to bowl sides out, and among his 52 wickets for the season there were several match-winning performances, including a bamboozling spell against Middlesex when no fewer than 4 of his 6 wickets were caught by Rohan Kanhai at slip off the 'arm ball', which they simply couldn't pick.

The fact that some of the innings I played that summer contributed to our overall triumph was a source of great pride. For someone who had lived and breathed Warwickshire County Cricket Club and Edgbaston almost from birth, being a part of the 1972 title-winning side means as much to me now as any of my hundred centuries or fifty England caps. It was also the inspiration and motivation for replicating that success when I became Warwickshire's chief executive twenty-two years later.

8

Babies, Breakthrough and Boycott

While inclusion in the England party for the winter tour of India, Pakistan and Sri Lanka was welcome reward for a successful summer, it came with a clear caveat. The England selectors had made it known publicly that this tour was Keith Fletcher's last chance to establish his credentials as an England batsman, and although I had not been 'put on watch' in quite the same way, I had played only a few Tests less than Keith, and my record was equally, if not more, unimpressive.

Family circumstances had also changed. I was now not only a husband but also a father and I was certainly not looking forward to being separated for four months from Jill and Becca, our little girl, who was just over a year old. So much changes so fast in the lives of small children, and with the tour lasting from the beginning of December to the end of March, I knew that I would miss the excitement of a family Christmas.

These days, of course, things have changed very much for the better and everything is done to ensure minimal disruption to family life. In 1972, however, there was a twenty-one-day limit on the length of time wives were permitted to be on tour with their husbands. They were regarded with huge suspicion by administrators, who seemed to believe that their presence would undermine the authority of the management and 'esprit de corps' among the players.

Throughout my Test career the twenty-one-day limit was a source of considerable tension between players and administrators. It also put marriages and relationships under unnecessary stresses and strains. Tony Greig was one of the most vocal opponents of what many of us saw as an entirely arbitrary regulation. He described it as 'an appalling encroachment on the privileges of every married man'.

There is little doubt in my mind that a ruling, supposedly designed to promote team spirit, was utterly counterproductive. In addition to creating much ill feeling, it also resulted in some of England's best players refusing to go on tour. I have little doubt that Alan Knott's decision not to go to Australia in 1979/80 was influenced by Peter May's refusal to allow his family to join him for the second half of the trip. In addition, Graham Gooch made it perfectly clear that his decision to withdraw from the 1986/87 Ashes series was in order to spend more time with his young family.

If evidence was needed that sportsmen and women are happier and more relaxed when they are not separated from their families it was provided by Kerry Packer and World Series Cricket (WSC) between 1977 and 1979. Having consulted with the players, he liberalised the whole system, leaving it up to individuals to decide how, where and when to share time with their loved ones.

Sadly, when peace was finally made between WSC and the game's establishment, Kerry Packer's enlightened approach to families was abandoned, along with many of his more imaginative innovations. In fact, one of the things I am most proud of was that, in the early days of my joining the England and Wales Cricket Board (ECB), we changed the regulations so that players and their families were no longer separated for such cruelly long periods of time.

The reforms paid off with the 2010/11 Ashes tour. Prior to departure there was full consultation with wives and girlfriends about how best to integrate family life with the drive for success on the field. The fact that England sealed a 3–1 series victory – the first Ashes triumph Down Under in twenty-four years – says it all.

By stark contrast, when I said my farewells to Jill and Becca before flying to Delhi as a member of the 1972/73 MCC touring party to India and Pakistan, it was the last time that I saw them for four long months. While the practicality of taking a 1-year-old child to India and Pakistan was one reason why Jill didn't join me for the twenty-one days that were allowed, the fact that there was no financial assistance with flights, hotels or expenses was another key factor, particularly as cricketers' salaries in those days were modest in comparison to the remuneration on offer today. Because of this, the only contact I had with Jill was a weekly exchange of airmail letters, and a telephone call on Christmas Day that had to be booked weeks in advance.

Although we began well in India with a 6-wicket victory in the First Test in Delhi, we eventually lost the 5-match series 2–1. On pitches that turned sharply their spin-bowling attack of Bedi, Chandrasekhar, Prasanna and Venkataraghavan was the decisive factor. It was, however, by no means all gloom and doom, and several members of the touring party acquitted themselves well. Not least among them was my old Essex mate Keith Fletcher, whose match-saving century in the final Test in Bombay, together with 97 not out at Madras and another half-century at Kanpur, made it clear to anyone who'd ever had any doubts that he was a batsman of genuine Test class.

My fortunes in India were more mixed. Having batted well for 46 in the first innings of the opening Test in Delhi, I lost confidence and form, which wasn't helped by an unfortunate event during the Second Test in Calcutta. The wicket turned from the first ball of the match and by the time we began our second innings the surface was so responsive to spin that the Indian left-arm seamer Eknath Solkar was given just one over with the new ball before being replaced by Bishan Bedi.

I opened the innings with Lancashire's Barry Wood and, having applied myself with caution, care and increasing confidence for half an hour or more, I played and missed at a delivery from Bishan Bedi that turned and bounced. Whether there was a noise from my bat hitting the ground or not I don't know, but as the ball passed the outside edge of my bat there was immediately a huge appeal behind me from wicketkeeper Farokh Engineer.

Before I could look up at the umpire, the jubilant eruption of the 100,000 Indian supporters in the crowd made me only too aware of my fate. Unable to hide my disappointment, I stood for a moment, open-mouthed, looking up the wicket towards the umpire, then back down at my bat before slowly setting off for the long trudge back to the pavilion.

I thought no more of it until the evening when I was summoned to manager Donald Carr's hotel room. 'I want to discuss the dissent that you demonstrated out on the field today,' he said.

'I didn't show any dissent, Manager,' I replied. 'I was disappointed to be given out. I didn't hit it.'

'Whether you hit it or not is immaterial,' he continued. 'If I see you do anything like that again in the future I shall make it my personal business to ensure that you never play for England again.'

I left Donald Carr's room feeling stunned and indignant; not only had I suffered at the hands of a terrible umpiring decision but I also felt that I had been treated unjustly. What's more, Donald's dressing-down seemed doubly harsh as he was usually so mild-mannered and courteous.

It was only on reflection that I came to appreciate the full context of the situation. Riots sparked by controversial decisions have not been unknown on Test grounds in India over the years and, with passions running high in a crowd of 100,000 at Calcutta, Donald Carr knew that even the slightest sign of dissent had the potential to spark off ugly scenes.

I also suspect that there was a distinctly personal element in his determination to avoid any sort of controversy on the subcontinent. In 1955/56, as captain of an MCC team to Pakistan, he had personally been involved in an incident involving an umpire which had almost led to the tour being called off, and ended his own international career.

To be fair to Donald, he never referred to the incident again and he was the first to congratulate me when my big breakthrough in Test cricket came a few weeks later in Pakistan. Before we left India, however, I experienced an act of generosity and sportsmanship that would be quite unthinkable in the modern game.

Having been left out of the last Test in Bombay, I was keen to have some net practice prior to the Pakistan leg of the tour, as I wanted to get back into some kind of form. Unfortunately, however, there were no such facilities available at the ground, and so I faced the frustrating prospect of kicking my heels for five days. At the end of the first day's play, Bishan Bedi, who had heard of my dilemma, approached me with a quite extraordinary offer. 'We'll bowl at you on the outfield if you like, Dennis,' he said.

Within half an hour he had arranged for a back net to be put up on the edge of the square, and I was padded up and ready to face Bishan, Venkat and Prasanna. They set an imaginary field in order to simulate match conditions, and then bowled at me for the best part of an hour.

After a day of sitting in the pavilion watching their batsmen compile a big score it was a good workout for the Indian spinners as well as for me, but it also demonstrated very clearly the excellent spirit in which the series was played, and the personal warmth between the players on both sides. The only proviso that the Indian management made in agreeing to give me some practice was that I was not to face Chandrasekhar, for fear that I would learn to pick his mystery 'googly'.

Even though I hadn't scored as many runs as I would have liked, I was sorry to leave India. What's more, I was apprehensive about our trip to Pakistan because of the political tensions in the country, and my fears intensified when we arrived in Karachi to discover that an anonymous letter had been sent to the team management with a message saying: 'Do not play Amiss in Pakistan.'

I have no doubt that it would have been dismissed as the work of a crackpot, except for the fact that the letter was signed 'BS'. This raised serious concerns that the source might have been the militant Black September group, which had been responsible for the assassination of the Jordanian prime minister and the massacre of eleven Israeli athletes during the 1972 Munich Olympics.

Whoever had sent the letter, the consequence of its arrival was that I was given a bodyguard for the entirety of the tour. This turned out to be less reassuring than it might sound because, although his role was to protect me twenty-four hours a day, he disappeared for significant periods – which always seemed to coincide with times when I was on the field of play and most at risk from anyone who wished me harm.

In addition to the insecurity generated by the anonymous letter, we also had to contend with an increasingly tense situation. Zulfiqar Ali Bhutto had recently become prime minister of the country and was attempting to introduce a new constitution to guarantee the future of Pakistan as a fully democratic republic. Feelings were running high as the country had been run by a succession of repressive military dictatorships for many years.

A few days before we arrived for the Third (and final) Test against Pakistan in Karachi, there had been a series of demonstrations orchestrated by student organisations pressing for more radical constitutional changes than Bhutto was proposing. As a result they had taken control of the city and the student leaders insisted that there would be no Test match unless they were in charge of running it.

Perhaps not surprisingly, there were utterly chaotic scenes when we arrived at the ground for the first day of the match. Students were all over the outfield and, as I went for a 'skier' catch during a warm-up fielding practice, I collided with one of them, splitting open a blood vessel on my forehead such that my face and shirt were covered in blood. I was immediately taken to the medical room to be treated by a doctor who was so elderly that he looked as though he should have retired at least twenty-five years previously. Just as this ancient medic pulled the first suture tight in the process of stitching up the open wound on my forehead, however, he seized his stomach and fell to the floor screaming.

The poor man had a hernia which had not only dropped but also twisted. While he was stretchered off to hospital for major abdominal surgery a replacement doctor was found to finish stitching me up. As if this wasn't enough, we subsequently discovered that after the operation the poor aged doctor had contracted a serious infection, leading to septicaemia and six more months in hospital.

In spite of all the drama, the cricket could not have gone better from a personal point of view. I scored my first Test century in the opening match of the series at Lahore. I followed this up soon after with 150 in the game in Hyderabad, and then scored more runs in the final game in the series in Karachi, when amazingly, along with Mushtaq Mohammed and Majid Khan, I was one of three batsmen in the match to be dismissed for 99.

Yes, the wickets in Pakistan had been absolutely perfect for batting, but before the 1972/73 tour it had been self-doubt and insecurity that had defeated me rather than the state of the pitch or the quality of the opposition bowlers. To make three big scores in successive matches at this level was the psychological breakthrough that I needed to succeed consistently as a Test batsman.

On arrival back in England, after four long months away, my primary focus was on spending time with the family and renewing my acquaintance with Becca, who was now 19 months old and a delightful bundle of energy and curiosity. Perhaps not surprisingly, she was initially puzzled by the sudden appearance of a stranger whose only role seemed to be to rob her of her mother's exclusive attention. What's more, the fact that her ever-expanding vocabulary did not include the words 'dad', 'daddy' or 'dadda' had a real and lasting impact. From that moment on, I did all I could to ensure that I was never again separated from Jill and our children for such a long period of time.

Meanwhile, there was no let-up in the demands of the cricketing calendar, and within a few weeks of my homecoming the New Zealand touring party arrived in England for a 3-match series. Led by the taciturn and wily Bevan Congdon, they were probably the strongest Kiwi side to have visited the UK. With players of the quality of Richard Hadlee, Glenn Turner, Brian Taylor, Hedley Howarth and Congdon himself, they were going to be no pushover.

With the West Indies arriving to play three further Test matches in the second half of the summer, the cricketing media viewed the New Zealanders, patronisingly, as something of a warm-up act. The reality was that, while we eventually won the series 2–0, we only achieved real dominance in the Third Test when typically overcast conditions and a green wicket at Headingley suited the swing and seam of Geoff Arnold, John Snow and Chris Old perfectly.

My success as an opener in Pakistan ensured my place in the side for the First Test at Trent Bridge, where my opening partner was Geoff Boycott. For all the accusations of selfishness, he was undoubtedly

England's best and most reliable batsman. Although not the most naturally talented player of his generation, he was nonetheless a superb technician and a real fighter whose qualities I came to admire the more I batted with him.

Having said that, our relationship got off to a decidedly shaky start. It all began when I had a conversation with MJK Smith during a County Championship match a few days prior to the opening Test against New Zealand.

'A few words of advice,' he said. 'You'll be opening with Geoff Boycott at Trent Bridge and you need to be careful. He's notorious for running his batting partners out and with the form you're in at the moment it would be a real waste. There are plenty of other ways to get yourself dismissed without any help from Geoff.'

Our first innings together at Trent Bridge went without incident as we put on just short of 100 for the first wicket. In the second innings, however, after Geoffrey had played out the first over from Richard Hadlee, I faced the left-arm pace of Dick Collinge. He pitched the first delivery up and I pushed it towards a gap at mid-off and immediately shouted 'run'. As Geoff and I passed each other I told him that there two runs to be had.

What I hadn't seen was the electric heels of Vic Pollard closing in on the ball from cover. It was only after I turned at the bowler's end, and taken four or five paces on my way back for the second run, that I could see that Vic already had the ball in his hand. 'No, no, no,' I shouted urgently. 'Go back, go back, go back.'

But Geoffrey kept on coming and, just as he was just about to overtake me, MJK's cautionary advice came flooding back. I instantly turned and grounded my bat behind the crease and poor Geoffrey was the man run out.

The flow of vernacular language that followed would have filled a dictionary of expletives, and even allowing for the broad Yorkshire dialect, there were several words and phrases that neither I, the umpires nor the eleven New Zealand fielders had ever heard before. My only consolation was that my parents weren't able to hear Geoffrey's vehement assertion that I had been born out of wedlock.

To rub salt into my Yorkshire friend's wounds, I went on to score an undefeated century. Meanwhile, by all accounts, Geoffrey sat in the corner of the dressing room cursing me and vowing that he would get his revenge. 'Look at that bugger out there, scoring all my runs,' he was reported as saying. 'I'll get him back. You'll see if I don't.'

When I discovered Geoffrey had told all and sundry that he planned to run me out deliberately in the Second Test at Lord's, I felt I had no option but to take the matter up with our skipper, Ray Illingworth, who, to his great credit, took the matter seriously. As a consequence, it was decided that Geoffrey and I should meet to resolve the matter together with the skipper after the team dinner on the evening before the Test was due to start.

The dinner was duly held in the committee room at Lord's, and when it was finished Raymond summoned us both to join him outside. All the other players, who were by now well aware of our contretemps, flocked to the door to hear what was going to be said. Geoffrey, however, pro-ceeded to make his way down the stairs making it quite clear how he felt about participating in any peace negotiations. 'I'm not staying to listen to any of this,' he said. 'I'm the one who got run out. Dennis is just being selfish pointing the finger at me.'

But before Geoffrey could take another step down the stairs, Raymond revealed the steely determination and authority that had galvanised England's success in the 1970/71 Ashes series. 'Geoffrey, get back up these stairs and sort this out now,' he said, before taking a brief pause. 'If you don't, you will never play for England again as long as I am captain.'

The response was instant, and, albeit reluctantly, Geoffrey returned. Within a quarter of an hour or so, he grudgingly agreed to a ceasefire. 'All right then, I promise,' he said. 'I won't run him out – not on purpose anyway.'

As with so many conflicts, it was to be some time before full diplomatic relations were resumed and the next day at Lord's, after we had won the toss and elected to bat, Geoffrey raced out of the pavilion well ahead of me, making it quite plain that he was not prepared to walk out to the wicket alongside me. It was a protest that continued throughout the summer with the result that I began to feel like the Duke of Edinburgh, forever walking in the shadow of Her Majesty the Queen.

Curiously enough, the conflict did not have any discernible impact on our effectiveness as an opening pair. Quite the reverse, in fact: during the 1973 summer we shared five first-wicket partnerships exceeding 50, two of which were well over 100. That's not to say that my nerves didn't jangle from time to time when Geoffrey called for a particularly sharp single, but I dare say that he was equally wary of my judgement.

Geoffrey is not a man who changes his mind easily, and I have no doubt that, even though almost fifty years have passed since our contretemps, he still believes he would have been justified in running me out. Nevertheless, we have developed a friendship that I would have thought impossible given the animosity we both felt at the time. In fact, Jill and I have stayed with Geoffrey and his wife Rachael at their beautiful home in Pearl Valley outside Cape Town in South Africa. It's not that either of us have forgotten the events of 1973 but rather that, over the years, they have become a source of mutual leg-pulling and good-humoured banter.

In the ten months following our truce at Lord's, our cricketing lives were taken up with no fewer than eight Test matches against the West Indies: three played in the home series that followed on from our victory over the New Zealand tourists and five on our tour of the Caribbean during the following winter. With Garry Sobers still at the top of his game and leading an emerging crop of exciting new talent, we knew that we faced a significant challenge.

Even though we were beaten conclusively in the First Test at the Oval by 158 runs, it wasn't until the fourth day of the following match at Edgbaston that I realised just how far we had to go to compete with the West Indies on level terms. It was when they were well into their second innings; with lunch due, our two spinners, Raymond Illingworth and Derek Underwood, were doing a good job in containing the attacking instincts and flair of Clive Lloyd and Garry Sobers.

As we came into the pavilion for lunch with the new ball due immediately after resumption, my Warwickshire colleague David Brown, who had been watching the morning's play, called me over. 'The wicket's really flattened out, Dennis,' he said. 'You must tell Raymond not to take the new ball. Mark my words – it'll disappear to all parts of Birmingham.'

No one knew more about bowling with a new ball on flat Edgbaston pitches than David Brown, so I duly passed on his message to Raymond Illingworth.

Ten minutes later, as we walked out to begin the afternoon session, the skipper handed a gleaming cherry-red ball to Geoff Arnold and instructed Chris Old to warm up in preparation for bowling the second over of the afternoon.

Within three overs the new ball looked more like an exploding hand grenade than the shiny orb the umpires had handed to Raymond. For the next forty-five minutes we witnessed attacking stroke play of breathtaking daring and scintillating brilliance, as both Garry Sobers and Clive Lloyd were particularly severe on Chris Old. Indeed, the young Yorkshire fast bowler's confidence seemed to evaporate along with control of line and length as they drove, pulled and cut him out of the attack. Tony Greig, who replaced him, was equally unable to halt the onslaught. Even with three men out on the off-side boundary, the West Indian left-handers struck the ball with such power that all the boundary fielders were bisected without any time to move.

To use a cinematic analogy, though, the utter dominance that Sobers and Lloyd achieved over our bowling attack during that session at Edgbaston was little more than a trailer for the feature-length film at Lord's. Here it was Rohan Kanhai, Garry Sobers and Bernard Julien who put us to the sword; all three made blistering centuries as the West Indies amassed a colossal 652–8 declared in their first innings.

After a humiliating defeat by an innings and 226 runs, a change of direction and leadership was widely called for. At 41 years old, Raymond must have known that his playing days were numbered and, with the press claiming that our success against New Zealand earlier in the summer had been little more than a 'false dawn', it was inevitable that we would have a new captain for the winter tour of the Caribbean.

Ray Illingworth was the fourth skipper I had played under at Test level after Brian Close, Colin Cowdrey and Tony Lewis. More than any of them, he had earned his place in England's cricketing history through the quality of his leadership during the 1970/71 Ashes win in Australia. I was genuinely sad to see him go, not least because of the way he had supported me over the 'run out' affair, even though Geoffrey Boycott was a fellow Yorkshireman and one of his long-standing teammates.

I had previously witnessed the strength of Raymond's leadership following an incident in the 1971 Lord's Test against India. John Snow found himself mired in controversy after he had, apparently, deliberately knocked Sunil Gavaskar over as he attempted to go for a run. The fact that Snowy had then tossed the Indian his bat in a casual and unapologetic manner had further incensed the Lord's establishment.

Almost as soon as we got back to the pavilion at the end of play, Billy Griffiths, secretary of MCC, burst into the dressing room and proceeded to harang Snowy: 'That was the most disgraceful thing I've seen on a cricket field,' he declared.

Raymond, however, was having none of it. As skipper he believed it was his responsibility to deal with Snowy, and – irrespective of the rights and wrongs of the matter – there was no way he was going to allow one of his players to be publicly rebuked and humiliated. 'This is neither the time nor the place, Billy,' he said. 'I'd be grateful if you would leave the dressing room and let me deal with this.'

The fact that Billy Griffiths not only complied with the request to leave but subsequently apologised for his intrusion spoke volumes about Raymond's authority and the respect in which he was held at the highest level.

To return to the summer of 1973, however, my personal contribution during the season ensured my selection for the winter touring party. While my undefeated hundred against New Zealand at Trent Bridge had set up the platform for our eventual victory I was, in many ways, more proud of the way I had been able to stand up consistently to the firepower and variety of the West Indies attack, and while we had been outplayed as a team for most of the series, my 86 not out in the second innings at Edgbaston ensured that we didn't suffer the humiliation of a whitewash on home soil.

9

Caribbean, Crisis, Craft and Consolidation

As the England touring party gathered at Heathrow on a cold, wet January morning in 1974, there seemed no better time to be jetting off for three months to the sunshine of the Caribbean. Although we were all going to miss our homes and families, it was hard to feel sad at the prospect of leaving behind a country suffering from rampant inflation, industrial unrest and the power cuts that had come with the recent imposition of a three-day working week.

Turmoil in Britain was such that, within weeks of our departure for the West Indies, the electorate had followed the example set by the England cricket selectors just a few months before and voted for a change of leadership. Thus, as Harold Wilson's new Labour government replaced Ted Heath's tired and demoralised Conservative administration, Mike Denness was chosen to halt the downward slide that seemed to have set in towards the end of Raymond Illingworth's tenure as England skipper. Even though he had only been captain of Kent for two seasons, Mike had already had a real impact in making the Hoppers one of the most successful teams in the country in all forms of the game.

At 33, Geoffrey Boycott was the oldest member of the touring party, with fast bowler Bob Willis, ten years his junior, the youngest by some margin. With the majority of the squad aged between 26 and 30, we seemed to have the perfect blend of youth and experience that would be needed to challenge the West Indies under the new leadership of my Warwickshire teammate Rohan Kanhai.

We were, however, in no doubt about the scale of the task that lay ahead; defeating the West Indies on home soil would not be easy, and we were all aware that the success of Colin Cowdrey's team in the Caribbean in 1967/68 had been less to do with cricketing dominance than Garry Sobers's over-generous declaration in the decisive Fourth Test.

Preparations for the First Test at the Queens Park Oval, Port of Spain, could not have gone better. In our warm-up games against the West Indies Board President's XI in Barbados, followed by a match against Trinidad and Tobago, everyone was in good form with the bat; Geoffrey Boycott got a double-century, Tony Greig and I both got hundreds, and all the other front-line batsmen spent much-needed time in the middle, getting at least one half-century each. The bowlers, too, looked fit and ready for the campaign ahead; Bob Willis, Chris Old, Geoff Arnold and Mike Hendrick all took wickets with some impressive spells of bowling.

Competition for places was fierce, and on the eve of the First Test no one envied the selection committee's task. The problem they faced was who to leave out, and there was particular sympathy for my Warwickshire teammate John Jameson when his name was excluded from the team sheet. He had batted superbly for a typically pugnacious 87 against the West Indies Board President's XI. Lancashire's Frank Hayes, who had similarly impressed in the Trinidad and Tobago match, got the nod ahead of him, and so it was John who had the thankless task of carrying the drinks for five days.

In spite of all our excellent preparations and collective optimism, however, the first morning of the match was a disaster. Whether it was humidity conducive to swing, early morning moisture in the pitch or simply our nervousness on the first morning of a big game, I don't know, but whatever the reason, by mid-afternoon on the first day of the opening match of the series in Port of Spain we were all out for a paltry 131.

By the end of the second day, however, our dismal batting display in the first innings was almost entirely overshadowed by a controversial incident that put the continuation of the match, and the remainder of the tour, in jeopardy. As the end of the day approached, the West Indies had reached 274–6 with Alvin Kallicharan going well on 142 not out. Derek Underwood was bowling the final over at Bernard Julien, who patted back the first five deliveries without drama or incident. He duly repeated his forward defensive to the last ball of the day and played it gently along the ground to Tony Greig, who was fielding close in on the off side. Before the umpire could call 'time' on the day's play, Alvin Kallicharan, at the non-striker's end, instinctively began walking off towards the pavilion without grounding his bat behind the crease. Greigy instantly threw down the stumps at the bowler's end and leaped in the air appealing for all he was worth. With Kallicharan well out of his ground, the umpire had no choice but to raise his finger and give him out.

The result was absolute mayhem. Kallicharan was understandably furious, storming off the field and smashing his bat on the stairs on his way back up to the West Indies dressing room. An ugly mood was also developing in the crowd, and we left the field to ominous jeering and voices crying out for revenge on Greigy; he was typically unrepentant, however, and on arrival back in the dressing room sought to justify his actions. 'You'd have both done exactly the same,' he said to Keith Fletcher and me, who happened to be changing beside him.

'Oh no we wouldn't,' we replied almost in unison.

And although the rest of the team also agreed that Greigy had crossed the invisible line between high-level competitiveness and sharp practice, he was, nonetheless, our teammate and we feared for his safety. We were also acutely aware that the sensitivities of the situation had been heightened because of his South African heritage. Indeed, there had already been barbed references in the Caribbean press prior to this crisis which falsely implied that he was a lifelong supporter of the apartheid system.

As large numbers of angry people surrounded the pavilion, our manager, Donald Carr, began discussions with officials at the ground about how to get Greigy back to the team hotel in safety. Before any conclusions could be reached, however, the door to our dressing room opened and in walked Garry Sobers.

'Things are in danger of turning really nasty out there,' he said. 'So I've decided that the best thing is for me to drive Greigy back to the hotel in my car.'

It was an extraordinary act of generosity from the greatest all-round cricketer the world has ever seen. What's more, given the tensions that were mounting in and around the ground, Garry Sobers was probably the only person in the Caribbean who could have got Greigy home safely that night. Garry was held in such high regard across the West Indies that no one would have dreamed of touching him or anyone travelling with him.

The matter didn't end there; there were numerous phone calls overnight back and forth between Lord's and the West Indies cricket administrators. Both parties were keen to find some sort of diplomatic agreement that would avert further escalation of the crisis and reassert the values of sportsmanship and fair play. The solution was clear for all to see the following morning when Bernard Julien walked out to bat alongside Alvin Kallicharan; he had been reinstated following the England management's agreement to withdraw Greigy's appeal.

Before we began our second innings we had much to reflect on. We sat in the dressing room, mulling over the reasons for our first-innings batting collapse, before Mike Denness asked a question that got right to the heart of the matter. 'Are we going to allow one poor performance with the bat to dominate the tone of the rest of this series?'

There was an almost simultaneous response from everyone in the squad. 'No way!'; 'Let's show 'em what we're made of'; 'The fightback starts here and now.'

The change of focus within the England camp was palpable, and by the end of the second innings we had taken a significant psychological step forward, having equalled the West Indies' first-innings tally of 392. Even though this was not enough to prevent an eventual West Indian victory by 7 wickets, we left Trinidad knowing that, as a team, we could match our opponents run for run and man for man.

Rarely in my experience has the impact of team unity been more evident than in our response to defeat in the First Test in Port of Spain.

There was no finger pointing or individual blame for our dismal batting performance in the first innings, nor did anyone refer to the 'Alvin Kallicharan Affair' again, other than in a humorous context. The emphasis of our team discussions from there on was on how we could achieve success in the next match. There was no dwelling on failure or disappointment, and this positive approach was central to inspiring both a collective renewal of purpose and a determination in each one of us, individually, to produce the goods when necessary.

As it happened, my own confidence had already received a significant boost in the second innings in Port of Spain when I'd gone past my previous highest Test score. What I didn't know as I walked back to the pavilion in Port of Spain, having been trapped lbw by Garry Sobers for 174, was that my new personal record would last for less than a fortnight.

In the imaginary games I had played endlessly in the back garden as a little boy, the countless centuries I had scored for England had always been against Australia in a winning cause. As far as my childhood imagination was concerned, nothing could be more thrilling than scoring a hundred against the clock at Lord's, or better still Edgbaston, to win the Ashes in a single-handed display of attacking brilliance.

The challenge that Geoffrey Boycott and I faced as we walked out to the wicket in the second innings of the Second Test in Jamaica, however, was nowhere near as romantic. Far from chasing a target to win the match, we had to set about the long slog of overhauling a deficit of 230 runs to avoid an innings defeat.

Our innings began immediately after lunch on the fourth day of the match, and it wasn't until almost ten hours later at the close of play on the fifth day, with the score on 432–9, that I finally walked off the field with 262 not out to my name. In actual fact, I could have been in the shower a couple of hours earlier; we had already saved the match just before the tea interval on the final day. Bob Willis, however, who was batting with me at the time, was having none of it. 'I'm not getting out,' he said with a typical vehemence. 'There's no way I want to bowl at them again.'

After such a marathon effort I was equally determined to carry my bat, and so we battled on under the intense heat of the Caribbean sun until the close of play. And while a match-saving innings might not have captured the imagination of a 9- or 10-year-old Amiss, the 30-year-old version, hot and exhausted, sat in the dressing room at Sabina Park quietly chuffed to have risen to the challenge.

In the Third Test in Barbados it was Tony Greig and Keith Fletcher's turn to display the fighting spirit that had become central to the team's ethos. Their centuries, in the first and second innings respectively, were brilliantly supported by back-to-back counter-attacking half-centuries from the indomitable and enigmatic Alan Knott, who always seemed to produce his best performances when the pressure was at its most intense.

In my view, there has been no better wicketkeeper/batsman in the history of the game than Knotty. Like so many people who have been touched by genius, however, his delightfully idiosyncratic ways bordered at times on eccentricity and, as his roommate on several tours, I came to know his unusual pre-match preparations all too well.

His fastidious routine would begin at around 10 p.m. on the night before a game with the careful unfolding and laying out of his back warmer, together with the vest and cricket shirt that he would be wearing the following day. These would then be given pride of place in the hotel airing cupboard. There was no hurrying him, and the whole process, which was conducted in an almost ceremonial manner, lasted until midnight. At 7 a.m. the next day he would be up and in the bathroom for a ritual of stretching and ablutions that lasted for at least an hour, and sometimes went on for half an hour longer. As a result we were often late for the team bus, much to the irritation of the management.

Although Knotty was uniquely unorthodox and highly individual, it was hard to imagine an England cricket team taking the field without him. Nevertheless, there were a couple of events during the West Indies tour which nearly brought an end to his uninterrupted tenure in the side.

The first occasion was in St Lucia when rain had brought the cancellation of the day's play. I took the opportunity to have a sailing lesson. Knotty was watching from the shore and, just a few minutes after I returned to the pontoon and moored up the dinghy, he approached me. 'That looked like fun,' he said. 'Why don't you take me out sailing?'

I can't remember if I told him that the lesson I had just finished had been my first ever experience of handling a dinghy but, whatever was said, five minutes later we were flying along, on our way out to sea, with the help of a strong offshore wind.

Half an hour later, however, the wind had dropped and we sat becalmed with the current taking us ever further away from land. 'I think we should start heading back now, Den,' said Knotty.

All I could think of was what the papers would say the following morning; there'd be no mention of me, of course, as there were plenty of other batsmen to take my place. Knotty, however, was irreplaceable, and in my mind's eye I could clearly see the headlines: 'Engand's Greatest Ever Wicketkeeper Lost At Sea.'

Fortunately for English cricket the wind finally returned and, after a couple of hours of inexpert tacking, we made it back to the safety of shore.

Not long afterwards Knotty diced with death for the second time on the tour. It was on another rain-affected afternoon in Guyana; Geoff Arnold, Roger Tolchard, Greigy and I decided to play tennis on a hard court close to our hotel. Just as Geoff Arnold was about to serve, Knotty walked past and shouted 'no ball' in a jovial attempt to put Geoff off. Alas, the joke was on Knotty; while focusing on us play-ing tennis, he failed to notice a large hole in the ground, filled to the brim with water from a combination of heavy rainfall and a burst pipe. There was a loud splash as he disappeared from view, and we all raced to the hole's edge to haul him out: soaking wet, shocked and scratched, but otherwise unharmed.

After both these episodes I could only think that the Good Lord had come to the conclusion that there was little or no point in having Knotty in Heaven; his wicketkeeping was already as close to perfection as it gets.

Although both the Barbados Test and the subsequent rain-affected match in Georgetown, Guyana, were drawn, we had begun to gain a sig-nificant level of control in games. In the Fourth Test, for example, Greigy and I both got hundreds as we made our way to an overall first-innings total well in excess of 400.

The real turning point of the series, however, was just before the Second Test in Jamaica. Greigy had been having nightmares about bowling his medium-pace seamers on flat Caribbean pitches at Clive Lloyd. He was terrified that the great Guyanan left-hander would smash the ball back at him with such force as he followed through that he would be in danger of being decapitated. As a consequence, he decided to experiment with the bowling of slow-medium off-cutters.

The results of this change of style were initially decidedly mixed. He enjoyed little success in Barbados, and although he took 6 wickets in the Third Test at Barbados he proved very expensive. Every over he dragged down one or two deliveries short and wide of the off stump. The main beneficiary in Jamaica was Lawrence Rowe, who dispatched the ball with monotonous regularity to the square cover boundary as he stroked his way to a triple-century. Even allowing for the fact that we didn't place a man back on the cover fence until he got to 200, it was one of the finest and most commanding Test innings I have witnessed.

There are many players who would have shrunk back into the shadows after the mauling he got from Lawrence Rowe in Barbados, but not Greigy; he had an unerring self-belief and was one of the most fiercely competitive cricketers I played with or against throughout my career. Refusing to bow to the majority view in the media that he should revert to medium-pace seamers, Greigy soldiered on with his off-cutters, determined to prove his critics wrong.

As the controversial running out of Alvin Kallicharan in the First Test had revealed, Greigy's 'win at all costs' philosophy sometimes got the better of him, but by the time we arrived back in Port of Spain for the final Test of the series, he had more than made up for his impulsive error of judgement. Not only had he made significant contributions on the field with bat and ball, but he had also proved to be a brilliant tourist, full of sociable charm, vitality and good humour. It was in the final match of the series in Trinidad, however, that he surpassed everything else he'd achieved in the previous three months.

The match proved to be as nail-biting a contest as any I have ever played in. It was full of drama with lots of twists and turns and contrasts in fortune. On the West Indian side, for example, Alvin Kallicharan, who had batted so brilliantly in the First Test for 158, bagged a pair, while for England Geoffrey Boycott, who was devastated to be caught behind off Bernard Julien for 99 in the first innings, put disappointment to one side and made it to three figures in his second knock of the match. It was as fine an innings as Geoffrey had ever played, and it set us on course for victory.

There is a saying, however, that 'it's not the batsmen but the bowlers who win matches', and while I suspect the sentiment was first expressed by a bowler, there is no doubt in my mind that squaring the series in the West Indies was primarily because of Greigy's bowling success. In spite of everything, he had resolved to stick with his off-cutters, and in the final Test of the series in Port of Spain he proved his point.

Standing 6ft 6in tall, Greigy was able to release the ball from around 9ft high, adding steep bounce to the prodigious 'rip' he gave to each delivery with his unusually long, strong fingers. These elements, combined with his unshakeable confidence that every ball he bowled would be unplayable, made him a fearsome prospect, and when he got his tail up, so to speak, there was no stopping him. Taking 8–86 in the first innings and 5–70 in the second, he tore the heart out of a West Indies batting line-up that had dominated every other attack in world cricket.

His achievement is all the more impressive when compared to Lance Gibbs's performance on the same wicket in the same match. Generally regarded as the best off-spinner in the world, the West Indian was nowhere near as dangerous or effective as Greigy, whose 13 wickets far exceeded Lance Gibbs's tally of just 4.

From a personal point of view, the 1974 tour to the West Indies was by far the happiest and most successful of my career. Scoring two centuries and an undefeated double-hundred, I had batted with poise, technical skill and great stamina throughout the tour. As a consequence, I was now firmly established at the top of the order as Geoffrey Boycott's opening partner. More importantly, I was among a group of players whom I had come to regard as my best friends and who shared my ambition to get better and better.

10

Down Under, Disarray and Demoralised

Having squared the series against the odds, we returned home far tougher and more confident than we had been when we left England on that cold, wet January day three months before. Moreover, the progress we had made in the Caribbean seemed to be conclusively confirmed by a 3–0 thrashing of India during the first half of the English summer. Our batsmen dominated the series with two centuries from Mike Denness, one each from Keith Fletcher, Tony Greig, John Edrich and me, and a double-hundred in only his second Test from David Lloyd.

Our good form continued throughout the second half of the season, when we played a 3-match series against Pakistan. Although the games all ended disappointingly in draws, we had the best of the first two, but not the the final Test at the Oval when Zaheer Abbas established his status as a world-class batsman with a superlative double-century.

At the end of September, when the England selectors met at Lord's to pick the sixteen players for the winter tour of Australia, there was considerable optimism that we would repeat the success achieved Down Under four years previously by Raymond Illingworth's side.

As history reveals, we lost the 1974/75 series 4–1. Our defeat was so comprehensive, in fact, that there were even calls for a public enquiry to be established to explore how and why it all went so horribly wrong. More column inches in the media seemed to be devoted to analysis of the tour than any other topic of the day, including Margaret Thatcher's defeat of Ted Heath in the Conservative Party leadership election.

As far as the tour was concerned, the general consensus was that things had started to go awry almost from the word 'go'. Most of the senior players felt the selectors had made a serious mistake in omitting John Snow from the team. Not only was he still a potent force as one of the very few genuinely fast bowlers in the country, but on the Ashes-winning tour of 1970/71 he had established a significant psychological advantage over several of the leading Aussie batsmen, including the captain, Ian Chappell.

Snowy had been overlooked by the selectors during the series against India and Pakistan as punishment for bowling underarm earlier in the summer in a Test trial at Worcester. It was his way of protesting, not only at having to prove himself to the selectors, even though he'd already taken 150 Test wickets, but also because the wicket at New Road was so flat that he thought bowling properly was a waste of time and effort.

To give ourselves the best chance of winning in Australia we needed him in the side, and so Keith Fletcher, Tony Greig, Alan Knott, Derek Underwood and I met with Mike Denness and urged him to use all his influence as captain to persuade the selectors to let bygones be bygones and include Snowy in the touring party.

The story we subsequently heard was that the selection meeting was well under way, and Mike Denness was in the middle of arguing the case for picking Snowy as the number one strike bowler. All of a sudden, Gubby Allen marched into the room, unannounced and uninvited. Somehow or other, he had heard that there were groups lobbying for John Snow's selection, and he had arrived to make good and sure that they weren't successful.

In those days Gubby Allen regarded Lord's as his own fiefdom in a not dissimilar way to Sepp Blatter's autocratic control of FIFA. He had, over the years, held every senior administrative role in the game, including chairman of the England selectors, president and treasurer of MCC. While he no longer held office, he nonetheless still lived in a 'grace and favour' house behind Lord's, and, as a stockbroker, continued to have a significant influence on MCC's finances and investments. To all intents and purposes, he was the power behind the throne at Lord's. Thus, when he instructed the selectors not to take John Snow to Australia, they fell into line without argument.

As if going to Australia without our best bowler wasn't bad enough, we also had to 'make do' without our leading batsman, even if it was for very different reasons. Although originally selected for the trip, there were strong rumours within days of the touring party being announced that Geoffrey Boycott didn't want to go. The fact that he didn't rate Mike Denness as a captain was an open secret, and although the official reason given for his withdrawal was a wish to spend the winter preparing for his benefit, suspicions about his real motives remained. And because Geoffrey informed the selectors of his decision just days before our departure, Kent's Brian Luckhurst had to be summoned from a family holiday in Spain as a last-minute replacement.

There were also management issues arising during the tour that certainly didn't help the cause. Not least of these was the officious way in which the powers-that-be monitored the time we spent with our families. We were all well aware, of course, of the twenty-one-day regulation that governed the length of time we were allowed to have with our wives and children. On this trip, however, we were not trusted to deal with the matter ourselves, and our physiotherapist, Bernie 'the Bolt' Thomas, was deputed to keep an official count of the number of nights each player had spent with his family, and inform us when our twenty-one days were up.

This was a particular issue for Jill and me as there had been a recent addition to the Amiss family. Paul had been born less than three months before our departure, and having missed out on four crucial months of Becca's development while away in the West Indies, I was anxious to spend the three weeks that we had together in as relaxed a family atmosphere as possible. The constant reminders from Bernard Thomas of the days, hours and minutes that we had left was like having the Sword of Damocles hanging over our heads.

The problem was that Alec Bedser, the manager, was a confirmed bachelor who had no understanding of how intrusive it was to be monitored in this way. Indeed, there were times during the Australian tour when we felt that we had stepped into George Orwell's *1984* and that Big Brother was watching us.

Although a sound administrator and a magnificent bowler in his day, Alec was not a leader with the ability to inspire the troops and raise morale when the going got tough – as indeed it did in Australia. In truth, he was a thoroughly decent, hardworking man, but he lacked the common touch and any sense of spontaneity. This was perfectly illustrated by the fact that at each and every official function throughout the tour he told the same story about a racehorse owner without ever changing a single word, or adjusting his speed of delivery and intonation.

In the final analysis, though, the problems of team selection and the management issues were of minor consequence in comparison to the impact that Dennis Lillee and Jeff Thomson had on the series. Bowling on hard, fast, bouncing wickets at speeds consistently above 90 miles per hour, they proved a fearsome prospect. Even so, it was more than just raw pace that made the Aussie duo so lethal.

First and foremost, they operated as a pair, which meant that there was no let-up or respite from the intensity of their blistering assault from either end. In addition, like all great fast bowlers, they seemed to be driven by a primitive energy and need for physical and psychological supremacy. It was this, I believe, that fired the hostility and aggression that was in many ways far more intimidating than the speed at which they delivered the ball. Moreover, perhaps paradoxically, there were times when they appeared to be in competition as to which of them could have us ducking, diving and weaving more often. Indeed, it was hard not to think that they took as much pleasure in hitting us as in getting us out – both of which they did with monotonous regularity.

Not surprisingly, there were a significant number of media pundits who blamed the extraordinary success that Lillee and Thomson achieved in 1974/75 on defective batting techniques and a lack of courage. While I would not dispute that our batsmen were, for the most part, blown away by the quality of the Australian attack, I would also point to the following winter when a West Indies batting line-up that included Viv Richards, Clive Lloyd, Lawrence Rowe and Roy Fredericks was similarly steam-rollered by Lillee and Thomson in a 5–1 series hammering.

There were also suggestions that we could have done more to pre-pare for the onslaught that we encountered, and that, prior to departure, more time in the indoor nets at Lord's facing short-pitched bowling on a pitch of reduced length would have been beneficial. Ironically, it was something that we tried before the Fourth Test in Adelaide when AC Smith, our assistant manager, bowled a barrage of bouncers at us off 18 paces. All he succeeded in doing, however, was badly bruising Keith Fletcher's top hand.

In actual fact, we couldn't possibly have anticipated the 'Lillian Thomson' phenomenon. Before our arrival, Thommo had only ever played one previous Test match. It had been against Pakistan and he had failed to take a single wicket in the match and ended up with a first-innings bowling analysis of 0–100 off just 17 overs. Majid Khan and Sadiq Mohammed had taken a particular liking to him, dispatching an array of wildly directed deliveries to all corners of the Melbourne Cricket Ground.

Nor did it seem that there was any reason to be unduly concerned about Dennis Lillee; he had only recently returned to the game after fifteen months out with a serious back injury. While he had taken a few early-season wickets for Western Australia in the Sheffield Shield, he wasn't 'pulling up any trees', and the reports that we heard were that he was bowling at a brisk fast-medium off a greatly reduced run-up.

As it transpired, however, because Australia won the toss and batted in the First Test at Brisbane, it wasn't until the afternoon of the second day's play that we first experienced the reality of the situation. Indeed, as Brian Luckhurst and I walked out to open the innings, our first surprise was to see Dennis Lillee mark out his run-up.

'How much further back is he going?' Brian remarked, as Lillee strode purposefully towards the boundary.

'You can take the first ball if you fancy it,' I replied, but Brian was having none of it and so as I looked up, having taken my guard, there was Dennis Lillee no more than 10 yards from the sight screen, his foot scuffing at the ground like the wild bull of the Pampas, raring to unleash his first thunderbolt of the series.

After less than ten minutes any misapprehensions we might have had about the Australian strike force were completely dispelled. Two deliveries in Lillee's first over whistled past my nose, while at the other end Brian Luckhurst turned as pale as ash as Thommo's first delivery of the day flew past his forehead without him appearing to have seen it.

'You can't say you haven't been warned,' said Dennis Lillee at the end of another terrifying over.

And indeed, he had warned us in no uncertain terms. It had happened the previous day as he walked off the ground following his dismissal in Australia's first innings. The Aussies had got to about 230–8 and we were obviously anxious to finish them off quickly. Dennis Lillee, however, had other ideas, and proceeded to hang on for a further forty minutes or so in a hugely frustrating partnership with Max Walker. Greigy, who had reverted to bowling seamers on the unresponsive Brisbane pitch, got thoroughly fed up with this and, in spite of Lillee's status as a tailend batsman, bowled a fierce bouncer at him which Dennis could only fend off and stand watching as the ball looped up into the air and into the gloves of the ever alert Knotty.

'Don't forget who started this,' snarled Lillee on his way back to the pavilion.

'I won't,' retorted Greigy. 'Now f★★★ off back to the dressing room where you belong.'

Unfortunately for us, it was clear by the end of the Brisbane Test, during which Dennis Lillee and Jeff Thomson had shared no fewer than 13 wickets between them, that the only place either of them belonged was out in the middle, bowling Australia to victory. Moreover, while Greigy had delighted in firing the opening shot of the campaign by bouncing Dennis Lillee, the impact had been like shooting a pop gun compared to the exocets the Aussies launched back at us in return.

Throughout the series, Lillee and Thomson were backed up superbly by slip catching of the highest quality, with the Chappell brothers in particular hanging on to every chance that came their way. We also had a running commentary from Rod Marsh behind the stumps to contend with. A master in psychological warfare, Marshy was forever finding new ways to unsettle and intimidate us. When I was facing Jeff Thomson at Brisbane, for example, one of his bouncers flew through to Marshy behind the stumps; down on his haunches he went, as if he'd been dramatically felled by a bullet. 'My God,' he cried, loud enough for everyone in the ground to hear. 'That's the fastest ball I've ever taken in my life.'

'I know,' I yelled back. 'I don't need you to tell me!'

Another significant factor was the support that the crowds gave to the home team, and the blatant derison that the Aussie supporters always seem to reserve for the visiting Poms. While much of it was good-humoured, there were times when the jeering and verbal assaults became personal and abusive. I had experience of this during the Third Test at Melbourne. I was fielding on the boundary when one member of the crowd, with a particularly strident and raucous voice, started haranging me from the stands. 'Hey, Amiss!' he shouted. 'You're fielding's no better than your bloody batting. My 3-year-old in kindergarden's a better bloody cricketer than you are. You're the worst bloody player I've ever seen, and I've seen some bad ones!'

The man was relentless, and over after over I trudged back into position on the boundary edge to be greeted by yet another volley of abuse. Had I been scoring runs it would have been water off a duck's back, but with a run of disappointing scores behind me it wasn't so easy just to shrug it off.

Having put up with it for an entire session, I decided it was time for someone else in the team to take their turn, and so I asked Mike Denness if he could move me to somewhere else on the field. Instead of bringing me in to the inner ring of fielders, however, he sent me to field on the boundary on the other side of the ground, and I hadn't been there for more than a couple of overs when an all-too-familiar voice rang out from the stand behind me.

'Hey, Amiss!' he yelled. 'Remember me, mate!'

It seemed that there was no escape from either the relentless derision of the crowd or the fearsome pace of the Aussie attack. It was the greatest physical and psychological challenge that any of us had ever faced and, in truth, Greigy and Alan Knott were the only two of our batsmen to find a way of dealing with the steep bounce and pace generated by the Australian attack. Although they could not have been more different physically, Greigy an entire foot taller, they both adopted the batting technique of keeping leg side of the ball. This helped them avoid getting tucked up by the sharply bouncing ball. It also allowed them to free their arms and launch an off-side counter-attack.

Greigy gave a perfect display of this approach in the first innings at Brisbane where he struck seventeen 4s, mostly through square cover, on his way to an astonishing century. Typical of Greigy, he also found a way to get under the Aussies' skin. Every time he played an attacking shot off Dennis Lillee he shouted out comments like: 'That's another four,' and 'Go and fetch that one.' Dennis, who was seething with anger, proceeded to bowl faster and faster, temporarily losing his length and line.

In spite of Greigy's demonstrative display, however, the Aussie pacemen reigned supreme and the havoc that they wrought at Brisbane went beyond taking our wickets. A particularly vicious lifter from Jeff Thomson, for example, hit John Edrich so hard in the chest that two of his ribs were cracked, and I sustained a fracture of the right thumb, having been hit on the bottom hand by consecutive steeply bouncing deliveries, one from Dennis Lillee and the next, even faster, from Jeff Thomson.

With both John and me unfit for the Second Test, it was clear that a replacement batsman had to be summoned. The players felt unanimously that Basil D'Oliveira was the obvious choice. He was still one of the best players of fast bowling in England, but the management had other ideas and called up 42-year-old Colin Cowdrey, who had not played a Test for England for over three years. While there were jokes at the time about sending for 'Dad's Army', Colin probably did as well as Basil D'Oliveira or anyone else who might have been selected. His 42 at

Perth, having just got off the plane after a twenty-four-hour flight from London, showed real courage.

As the series progressed, however, Australia became more and more dominant and English successes fewer and far between. Indeed, the moments of hope were rare and short-lived. Although my hard-fought 90 in the Third Test at Melbourne, for example, enabled us to force a draw, any thought that I might have finally broken the Aussies' psychological hold over me was soon dashed; I bagged the second pair of my career against them in the next match at Adelaide.

While guts and determination were not enough to ward off the prospect of defeat, they were never in short supply. Knotty, for example, led the way in ensuring that we never gave up, scoring sparkling centuries with his highly unorthodox method in the Third and Fourth Tests. Irrepressibly chirpy and delightfully eccentric, he had a quip for almost every situation. After he had scored his second hundred in the series at Adelaide, for example, he came back into the dressing room and sat beside me.

'Well played, Knotty,' I said. 'That was a brilliant innings – a real joy to watch.'

'Cheers, Dennis,' he replied. 'But just remember, mate, it's far better to have arse than class but if you have both it really helps.'

If by 'arse' he meant spirit, courage, innovation and daring, then Knotty had those in spades and, combined with his immaculate wicketkeeping throughout the tour, he was our 'man of the series' by a country mile.

It wasn't until the Sixth and final Test of the series that we had any respite from the Aussies' unrelenting assault. Jeff Thomson, who had a side strain, was declared unfit, and for the first time in three months our batsmen had the psychological relief of not having to contend with supercharged pace from both ends. As if released from a stranglehold, most of the top-order batsmen scored runs in our one innings total of 529. Mike Denness, who had been the target of sustained media criticism throughout the tour for both his batting and captaincy, scored a brilliant century, as did Keith Fletcher. Tony Greig and John Edrich also pitched in with scores of 89 and 70 respectively.

It wasn't until we moved on to New Zealand that I personally felt the oppressive weight of Australia's yoke of pressure lifted from my shoulders, and while the undefeated century I scored in the Second Test in Christchurch did much to restore my shattered confidence, it didn't compensate for my feeling that I hadn't proved myself against the best in the world. Nor did it help me understand the fluctuating fortunes of the previous twelve months; from the zenith of success in the Caribbean to the nadir of my disappointment Down Under.

11

Crisis, Candour and Comeback

The most significant legacy of the 1974/75 Australian tour was the realisation that the best way to win Test matches was to pack the side with as many bowlers as possible who could deliver the ball consistently at above 90 miles per hour. Thus the era of the 'superquicks' was born, and from then until now, almost without exception, the no. 1 Test side in the world has been the one that has possessed the greatest number of out-and-out fast bowlers. Australia, for example, dominated the mid-1970s by including three, and often four, genuine pace bowlers when both Gary Gilmour and Lenny Pascoe were chosen in support of Lillee and Thomson. The West Indies side that knocked the Aussies off their perch and reigned supreme for the next ten years also opted for a 'fearsome four' who were selected in combination from a seemingly endless production line of superquicks; it began with Andy Roberts, Michael Holding, Wayne Daniel and Joel Garner, and was followed soon after by the blistering pace and bounce of Colin Croft, Patrick Patterson, Malcolm Marshall, Courtney Walsh and Curtly Ambrose.

The recognition in England that the only way to compete with the great Australian and West Indian teams of the 1970s and 1980s was to fight fire with fire was reflected in two initiatives set up to find supercharged fast bowlers. The first campaign was launched in 1983 by Ted Dexter and Bob Willis, and the second in 1997, with Dennis Lillee recruited as the judge and mentor. Although neither was successful in unearthing another Fred Trueman or Frank Tyson, the analysis of what the England Test team needed to become no. 1 in the modern game was absolutely right. This was clearly demonstrated in 2005 when Steve Harmison, Andrew 'Freddie' Flintoff, Simon Jones and Matthew Hoggard – the 'Four Horsemen of the Apocalypse' – bowled England to Ashes victory. Indeed, more than one respected pundit has suggested that the moment England achieved psychological dominance in the series was in the First Test at Lord's when a lightning-quick bouncer from Steve Harmison struck a resounding blow on Ricky Ponting's helmet.

Back in 1974/75, however, we did not have helmets to protect us against the very real threat of serious injury. Ironically, perhaps, the full reality of the physical danger we had faced in Australia only really dawned on us because of an incident that occurred during the first of two Tests that we played on the second leg of the 1974/75 tour in New Zealand.

It was late on the fourth afternoon of the Auckland Test, and New Zealand had been forced to follow on. With only one wicket left to fall, the Kiwis still required 105 runs to make us bat again. There was, how-ever, increasing frustration that we might not finish the game that night as Geoff Howarth kept sneaking a single off the fifth or sixth ball of every over to protect tailender Ewen Chatfield, who was making his Test debut.

With less than fifteen minutes to go to the close of play, Derek Underwood bowled a maiden at Howarth, leaving New Zealand's no. 11 to face a full over from Peter Lever. Having been narrowly missed at short leg off the first ball of the over, and played and missed at the next three, Ewen Chatfield completely misjudged the fifth ball that he faced. Turning his head away from a sharply rising, short-pitched delivery, he was struck on the right temple and immediately collapsed.

The seriousness of the injury was instantly apparent as poor Ewen lay on the ground twitching and moaning. Fortunately, Bernard Thomas, our physio, who had been feeling unwell and was originally not coming to the match, had arrived and came out together with a local St John's

Ambulance man. By this time, however, Ewen Chatfield had not only swallowed his tongue, but his heart had stopped beating. On being told that there was neither a doctor nor any medical equipment at the ground, Bernard took control of the situation and released Ewen's tongue from the back of his throat before beginning mouth-to-mouth resuscitation and a series of chest compressions.

Within half an hour Ewen was conscious and on his way to hospital where, thankfully, he made a full recovery. Even though he had sustained no lasting damage, there was no escaping the fact that in the several seconds it took Bernard to get Ewen's heart beating again, he had been technically dead.

Every batsman is, of course, aware of the danger of being hit and, in the days before helmets, there was a far greater risk of serious injury than exists today. For those of us who had spent the previous four months ducking and diving to avoid deliveries travelling at speeds well above anything Peter Lever could manage, witnessing the 'Ewan Chatfield incident' was a profoundly disturbing moment. From a personal point of view, the psychological scars from the Ashes series that had just begun to heal were opened up again, and lurking at the back of my mind, for months to come, was an unease that surfaced every time I walked out to the wicket to bat.

What I hadn't fully appreciated until the English domestic season began, shortly after our return from Australia, was that the battering we had received at the hands of Lillee and Thomson was the talk of cricket clubs and dressing rooms up and down the country. As a consequence, every county captain was only too aware of the legacy that I had brought home with me from Australia. In a match against Leicestershire, for example, Ray Illingworth shouted instructions at loudhailer volume to Norman McVicker that were clearly calculated to unnerve me. 'Come on Norman! Get stuck into Amiss early on. Bounce him.'

It was pretty much the same in all the County Championship matches that I played in 1975, with every fast bowler fancying his chances of unsettling me with a barrage of short-pitched deliveries. The very last thing I needed was another encounter with Lillee and Thomson but, with Australia due to arrive in May for a back-to-back series in England, that was precisely the prospect that awaited me.

Surprisingly, given the drubbing we had experienced in the winter, the team that the England selectors picked for the First Test at Edgbaston included only two players who had not been on the Australian tour. Not before time, John Snow was recalled from disciplinary banishment, and Graham Gooch was given a debut on the basis of terrific early-season form with Essex.

Perhaps predictably, it wasn't just the names on the England team sheet that were pretty much the same as during the Ashes tour: our performance was all too familiar as well. Nor were we helped by Alec Bedser's interference on the first morning of the match.

As the local boy I knew the Edgbasgton pitch well, and the wicket looked to me as though it would be slow and flat. Although not ideal for attacking strokeplay, it was likely to reduce the threat posed by the pace and bounce Lillee and Thomson had achieved on the hard Australian surfaces. Knowing that there was rain forecast for the next day that could liven the pitch up, it was clear to me and the other senior players that, if we won the toss, we should bat first. Alec Bedser, however, had other ideas. Focusing on the fact that the surface had a slight green tinge, he persuaded Mike Denness to put the Australians in – with disastrous consequences.

The Australians made their way to 359 on a lifeless, benign wicket before the rain duly came. Thereafter, we had to bat with the ball bouncing unpredictably and darting around in all directions. Dismissed for 101 and 173, we lost by an innings and 85 runs, with Dennis Lillee and Jeff Thomson taking 5-wicket hauls in the first and second innings respectively.

Mike Denness, who had clearly been living on borrowed time since the Ashes tour, was replaced as captain for the Second Test at Lord's by Tony Greig. In addition, David Steele was brought into the side to make his debut. Grey-haired, bespectacled and looking closer to 50 than his actual 34, Steeley seemed an unlikely choice for selection. He had a reputation for being a doggedly defensive and dull county professional, and no one had mentioned his name as being in contention for a place in the Test side.

In looking for the best person to blunt the Australian pace attack, Greigy had decided to consult his Sussex teammate, and England's best fast bowler, John Snow. 'Of all the batsmen in England currently playing county cricket, who plays you best?' he asked.

'David Steele,' Snowy replied without a second's hesitation. 'He may be a predominantly front-footed player, but he gets into line and never flinches, no matter what you throw at him.'

And what an inspired selection it was! It wasn't just that Steeley got runs every time he went to the wicket during that series; untainted by failure Down Under and looking more like an eccentric chemist than an international cricketer, he seemed to embody the British 'bulldog spirit' with his dogged refusal to allow the Aussie quicks to bully him into submission.

He also brought a touch of much-needed comic relief to proceedings. Stories about getting lost in the depths of the Lord's pavilion on his way out to bat in his first Test, and of his being sponsored by a butcher who promised to give him a lamb chop for every run he scored, tickled the nation's sense of humour. He became such a popular figure in fact that, later in the year, he won the public vote as BBC's Sports Personality of 1975.

Sadly, by contrast, had there been a vote for the Sports Failure of 1975 I would have been a strong contender. Having been dismissed 3 times in 4 innings by Dennis Lillee without getting past 10, I was discarded by the England selectors after the match at Lord's and returned to county cricket convinced that my Test career was over.

Perhaps it was the sheer relief of being released from the psychological knots that Dennis Lillee had tied me in, but in the very next match against Kent at Edgbaston I got a hundred and played with an expansive freedom that had been missing since the previous summer. In no time, the pleasure in playing and batting that had been squeezed out of my game by anxiety and apprehension began to return.

It was also my benefit year at Warwickshire and, at the age of 32, there was a deep temptation to opt for the easy life and play out the next three or four seasons in county cricket before joining the family business on a full-time basis. In tension with this, however, was the fact that I was increasingly being labelled as someone who 'couldn't play the quicks'. As a consequence I knew that I had something left to prove.

It would have been easy for me to duck the issue and ignore the fact that I had a problem. I was still getting a lot of runs in county cricket. In fact, between the beginning of 1975 and the end of the 1976 season I scored no fewer than twelve first-class centuries, including the fiftieth hundred of my career on 2 July 1976 against a Derbyshire attack that included Alan Ward, Eddie Barlow and Geoff Miller.

Never before in my life had I run away from the truth, and I wasn't about to start now. I knew there was something fundamentally wrong with my technique against the real quicks and although I was getting big hundreds on a regular basis against lots of very respectable county sides, when I came up against teams with genuine fast bowlers I had been found wanting. Andy Roberts for Hampshire and Imran Khan for Worcestershire, for instance, had both exploited my weakness against the short-pitched delivery, and dismissed me cheaply on a number of occasions.

If there were any doubts about the full extent of my batting Achilles heel, they were completely dispelled when I went in to bat for MCC against the 1976 West Indian tourists at Lord's. While my selection was recognition that I had been scoring runs consistently in county cricket, I knew that it was by no means indicative of a Test recall. I also knew that facing Andy Roberts, Michael Holding, Wayne Daniel and Vanburn Holder would be a completely different prospect from the day-to-day diet of county seam bowlers, particularly after the inflammatory remarks made by Tony Greig in a BBC radio interview before the tourists arrived.

'Are you looking forward to the series, Tony?' the interviewer had begun by asking.

'I most certainly am,' Greigy replied. 'I can't wait to get stuck in.'

'Excellent! Perhaps, though, you could give our listeners your assessment of the West Indies' qualities as a cricket side.'

'Well,' replied Tony. 'When they're up and winning they're great, but when they're down they really grovel.'

These were words that came back to haunt Greigy throughout the series. They also proved to be an inspiration to their battery of superfast bowlers who were only too keen to ensure that it was the England batsmen, and not they, who did the 'grovelling'.

The MCC match at Lord's provided the perfect showcase for Roberts and Holding to demonstrate their pace and hostility, and they steamed in to bowl at Mike Brearley and me when we came out to open MCC's innings. After dodging a series of skull-cracking bouncers by the finest of margins, I misjudged yet another short-pitched flyer which crunched into the back of my head, forcing me to retire.

I had broken the cardinal rule of batsmanship and taken my eye off the ball, just as Ewen Chatfield had done just over a year previously. The difference, however, was that he was a tailender while I was supposed to be a Test-class opening batsman, and so there was no escaping the reality that I either had to give up the lingering ambition of making a Test comeback, or address my technique against short-pitched, fast bowling.

I had tried the method adopted by Alan Knott and Tony Greig in Australia of staying leg side of the ball, but without success. In my case, when I moved inside and away from the line of the delivery, the distribution of my body weight was such that I was unable to get forward again if the ball was of full length.

The only other viable alternative was to experiment with the method that Ken Barrington had used to good effect against Wes Hall and Charlie Griffiths in the 1960s. Known as the 'Victor Sylvester' after the famous dancer, because of the finely balanced footwork, the technique involves taking your back foot back and across towards the off stump such that your head and eyes are lined up beneath the bowler's arm as it comes over. While the movement back allows you a critical fraction of a second longer to pick up the length and line of the ball, the balance and distribution of your weight does not prevent you from moving forward as normal if the ball is pitched up.

While coming up with a new technical approach is relatively easy, the real challenge always lies in developing and refining it, before going out into the middle to put it into practice under pressure. In this particular instance, I was supported by Warwickshire colleagues Andy Lloyd and Chris Maynard, who kindly agreed to bowl short-pitched deliveries at me in the indoor nets hour after hour, for days on end.

It didn't matter that Andy was an opening batsman and Chris a wicketkeeper. All I needed was for them to dig the ball in as short and fast as they could from 18 yards or so, and the hard bouncing surface in the indoor nets did the rest. Then, little by little, as the movement back and across became second nature, I grew increasingly adept at judging which ball to play and when to sway out of the way, allowing bouncer after bouncer to whistle harmlessly past my nose.

Not only did the 'Victor Sylvester' seem to give me that all-important extra millisecond within which to react, but getting my movement out of the way before the moment of delivery also ensured that I was completely still at the crease, with my eyes under the bowler's arm at the actual instant of release.

The first big test of my new technique came in early August at Hove in the Gillette Cup quarter-final against Sussex. The home side batted first and made 194 on a typically hard, green seaside wicket. As John Jameson and I arrived in the middle to begin our reply to Sussex's total, we could both clearly hear Tony Greig geeing up John Snow. 'Come on Snowy,' he cried in his guttural South African accent from first slip, 'get stuck into him. Knock his bloody head off.'

As I was the batsman about to take strike, there could be no doubt that the 'him' Greigy was referring to was me, and the head he was urging Snowy to decapitate was mine. It was soon all too apparent that Snowy meant business, and not only did his first ball whistle past the off stump almost before I'd brought my bat down, but the snarl that appeared on his face, as his top lip curled up on one side of his mouth, was an expression that I knew all too well. I'd seen it many times before when we'd played for England together, and I knew it was a sure sign that Snowy was in the mood to give it his all.

For the first time in eighteen months, however, I was completely unfazed by the short-pitched ball, confident enough to drop my hands and let those directed at my head or body go harmlessly through to the wicketkeeper. When Snowy dropped one short and wide of the off stump, I was quickly into position to crash it off the back foot to the square cover boundary; when he over-pitched, I was forward and driving him for three successive 4s in the arc between extra cover and midwicket.

After five expensive overs, Snowy snatched his sweater and trudged off to the fine-leg boundary, muttering dark oaths. He returned later in our innings to bowl three more overs with an equal lack of success as we blitzed our way to victory by 8 wickets, with 14 of the 60 overs remaining.

This was the moment when I really knew I was back. Greigy's telephone call to Jill the following day confirmed that he thought so too. 'Hello Jill,' he said, 'it's Greigy here.'

'Dennis isn't in, I'm afraid, Greigy,' she replied. 'He's at Edgbaston having a net.'

'No, Jill. It's you I want to talk to.'

'Me?'

'I want to ask what frame of mind Dennis is in. Do you think he's ready for a comeback?'

'You'd have to ask him, Greigy. You know you'd get a straight answer.'

'Yes – but I'm asking you. He got a brilliant 87 against us at Hove, and the way he played Snowy was fantastic – he took him to the cleaners. All I need to know is if his mind is in the right place for a comeback.'

I'm not sure how the conversation ended exactly, but the upshot was that I was recalled, after a year out of Test cricket, for the Fifth and final Test against the West Indies at the Oval.

With the tourists 2–0 up in the series, having won consecutive matches by conclusive margins, Greigy's depiction of a 'grovelling' West Indies side was looking increasingly absurd. Unabashed and undeterred, however, he continued to find ways of provoking a heated response from the opposition.

I found myself directly involved in one of Greigy's more demonstrative displays in our first innings at the Oval. The West Indies had already batted on a benign wicket as they compiled a colossal total of 687–8 declared. Even by ringing the changes, with no fewer than nine bowlers trying their luck, we couldn't slow the streaming salvo of boundaries rocketing from Viv Richards's bat, in particular, as he blazed his glorious way to 291.

Having lost my opening partner, Bob Woolmer, early on in our reply, David Steele and I set about seeing off the ferocity of Michael Holding and Andy Roberts, both of whom reached speeds well above 90 miles per hour. Roared on by the huge Caribbean contingent in the south London crowd, they peppered us with a barrage of bouncers and short-pitched rib crunchers without success.

For the best part of two hours we battled on against their four-pronged pace attack; when Holding and Roberts took a well-earned rest, their replacements were none other than Wayne Daniel and Vanburn Holder, whose fresh legs and lively pace ensured we had no respite from the full-on assault.

As we became more attuned to the pace, however, things began to change. It was almost imperceptible at first but, with a hundred partnership not far off, the crowd grew quieter and the number of bouncers per over reduced from three to two, and then again from two to one. Steeley's nudges and flicks for the occasional single became firmer pushes for twos and threes, and I found myself hitting the ball sweetly on both sides of the wicket.

After two hours of typically dogged determination, Steeley was lbw to a thunderbolt from Michael Holding, who then knocked out Chris Balderstone's middle stump without scoring just seven balls later.

Sensing capitulation, the Caribbean quicks ran in with renewed energy, as another blitz of bouncers began. But the incoming batsman – Peter Willey – was every bit as brave and obdurate as his former Northants colleague David Steele, and, once again, for the next two and a half hours we drew the sting out of the attack.

It was only when Peter played a tired shot to the medium pace of Collis King that the lull in the storm was over. Out of the pavilion stepped Greigy, swinging his bat like a drum majorette in a street parade and announcing at the top of his voice precisely what he was going to do to the West Indian attack.

'Right!' he cried, pumping himself up like a prize fighter. 'Now we're going to see some action. Come on Dennis, let's show them what we're made of. Let's get at them!'

'Calm down, Greigy,' I said as he marched towards me in the middle. 'We've just started to get on top of them; they were beginning to flag a bit. There's no need to stir them up. Let's keep it low key.'

But Greigy was never one to keep things low key. As he carried on declaiming how often and how far he was going to whack their 'quickies', Clive Lloyd summoned Michael Holding back into the attack from the Vauxhall End; he also waved towards Andy Roberts, who was resting down at fine leg, indicating that he wanted him to warm up for the next over from the Pavilion End.

With Holding and Roberts fully fired up, and the crowd baying for blood, we were once again ducking and swaying out of the way of three and sometimes four bouncers an over, while an unrepentant Greigy kept up his belligerent antics: 'Can't you bowl any quicker than that?' he shouted as another Holding exocet whistled past his nose.

The answer to the question came just a few balls later when Michael produced the yorker of all boot-crunching yorkers; it crashed at just under 100 miles per hour into Tony Greig's leg stump before he could bring his bat down. I actually had a moment of relief, as my instinct for self-preservation outweighed all other considerations. Never before had I been happy to see one of my own team members walking back to the pavilion.

Looking back on that match now I have very mixed feelings. On the one hand, I still feel keen disappointment at having been part of a heavily defeated team that was bowled out twice in three and a half days on a good batting pitch. Aside from that, however, I have a sense of deep satisfaction; I had overcome my demons and made a dramatic and successful return to Test cricket when hardly anyone believed it possible. Against the odds, I had found a way to play short-pitched fast bowling of the highest quality with confidence. Putting my new method into practice at the Oval, I had batted for over seven hours to reach my second double-century against the West Indies. To have achieved this while Michael Holding blew everyone else away, taking 14 wickets in the match, was a source of very special pride.

My good form continued in the winter with a stack of runs, including another Test century, during our 3–1 series victory over India. Nevertheless, within twelve months of my comeback double-hundred at the Oval, my Test career was over.

The end came, perhaps predictably, with successive low scores against the 1977 Australians, prompting EW Swanton to write that 'Amiss's magnificent marathon innings of 203 at the Oval against arguably the fastest bowlers the world has seen makes his disappointing performances against Australia all the more mystifying.'

Ironically, perhaps, it was the runs that my childhood hero, Denis Compton, scored against the 1953 Australians in such dashing style that I had always dreamed of emulating. Even so, when my international career came to an end, I had scored 11 centuries in 50 Tests at an average that was higher than several distinguished contemporaries, including Colin Cowdrey and Tom Graveney. As a 15-year-old starting out at Warwickshire, I'd have settled for that.

12

Rebellion, Rejection and Reconciliation

It was just over a month into the 1977 cricket season when rumours began to circulate that a group of the world's best players had been approached by Kerry Packer, the Australian media mogul. The story was that he was planning to set up a new organisation in competition with the game run by the established authorities. In dressing rooms around the county circuit there was much speculation about the names of the top players who might be joining his breakaway group. There was also talk that the players were being tempted by the promise of 'big money'.

At Warwickshire, as at every other county, there were a significant number of committee men, administrators and players confidently explaining why Kerry Packer's initiative couldn't and wouldn't get off the ground. A long list of reasons were given:

'What self-respecting cricketer is going to sacrifice their Test career to join some half-baked rebel organisation?'

'The International Cricket Council and the Test and County Cricket Board run the game and they simply won't let it happen.'

'When push comes to shove the players will see sense. Deep down they all know that the honour of playing for their country is far more important than financial reward.'

'Cricket is a traditional game and tradition always wins in the end. You'll see.'

Speculation gave way to reality towards the end of May, however, when an Australian newspaper owned by Kerry Packer officially announced the launch of WSC. The paper also confirmed the names of thirty-five top cricketers who had been signed for three years to play a combination of Test matches and one-day internationals for prize money equivalent to almost £1 million in today's money.

It wasn't the size of the financial rewards that shocked the cricketing establishment. The biggest stir was caused by the names of the star players who had committed themselves to the 'rebels'. The eighteen Australians who had signed included none other than their captain, Ian Chappell, his brother, Greg Chappell, Dennis Lillee, Jeff Thomson, Doug Walters, Rod Marsh and more or less every other player already in England for the 1977 Ashes series.

To rub salt into the ICC's wounds, the other seventeen players named were without doubt among the very best cricketers in the world at that time: they included Michael Holding, Viv Richards and Andy Roberts from the West Indies; Tony Greig, Alan Knott, John Snow and Derek Underwood from England; Maijd Khan, Imran Khan and Asif Iqbal from Pakistan; and Barry Richards, Mike Procter, Graham Pollock and Eddie Barlow from South Africa.

It also emerged that both Ian Chappell and Tony Greig had been actively involved in recruiting players on behalf of Kerry Packer while still in their respective roles as captains of Australia and England. The additional fact that Richie Benaud, a former Australian captain and long-time BBC cricket commentator, had been engaged by Packer to manage WSC prompted strong accusations of betrayal and treachery.

The immediate response of England's Cricket Council was to strip Tony Greig of the England captaincy for the forthcoming series against Australia. A statement was issued at the end of the council's emergency meeting saying that 'his action has inevitably impaired the trust which existed between the cricket authorities and the captain of the England side'.

Perhaps because my name wasn't on the initial list of those who had signed for WSC, people assumed that I shared the anti-Packer sentiment that was hardening around me. In actual fact, I felt more disappointment than anything else. During the previous two years I had been one of the leading run scorers in world cricket, and it was a blow to my pride, as much as anything else, that I hadn't yet been offered the chance to join the cricketing elite.

The fact that approaches to the England and Australia players had happened during the Centenary Test in Melbourne earlier in the year made my exclusion even more inexplicable. I had batted really well and shared in a partnership of over 160 with Derek Randall in one of the sternest tests of technique and temperament I had ever faced.

To digress for a moment: the background to my success in the Centenary Test was the perfect illustration of how important it is for sportsmen and women to be in the right frame of mind when they compete. We arrived in Australia from India with its low, slow pitches to play Western Australia on a fast, bouncy surface at Perth. Dennis Lillee, keen to establish a psychological advantage before the Centenary Test at Melbourne, had us swaying, ducking and diving in a typically hostile display that was an uncomfortable reminder of the 1974/75 series.

A couple of days after we arrived in Melbourne, however, I had a call out of the blue from a sports psychologist called Lee Saxon, who offered to help me break the mental stranglehold Dennis Lillee had over me by the use of hypnosis. On discovering that Lee was renowned for his work in helping leading football clubs win titles, I saw no harm in giving it a try.

In spite of some scepticism on my part, within minutes of the consultation beginning, Lee put me into a deep hypnotic state during which he introduced a whole series of positive words, phrases and statements. He also taped the session, and at the end of it he gave me a copy of the recording which I was instructed to play as often as possible before going out to bat.

The fact that, during the next few days, I pretended to the rest of the team that the headphones I was using were for listening to music is a clear indication of the fear that we all had in those days of showing any sign of weakness.

The attendance on the first day of the Centenary Test was close to 100,000 and as I walked out to bat at the MCG all I could hear was the crowd baying for blood, just as the packed Colosseum had done in Rome over a thousand years before when the lions were loosed on the gladiators: 'Kill, kill, kill! Come on Lillee – kill Amiss!'

As I approached the crease, however, the tape of my session with Lee Saxon played over and over again in my mind, drowning out all other sounds. 'You're a good player, Dennis. You got 90 the last time you batted against Lillee at Melbourne. You proved you could do it then and you're going to do it again today.'

In an effort to avoid the first ball that whistled past my nose at 90 miles per hour, I tumbled to the floor in an undignified heap. Once again the 100,000 crowd erupted in unison: 'Kill, kill, kill!'

But the tape played on in my mind, blocking out the hostility that filled the stadium, banishing self-doubt and fear of failure. 'I can do this. I know I can. I'm good enough. And that's why I'm here.'

And with that simple, clear, confident message ringing in my ears, I batted on to what should have been my first Test century against Australia. But having seen off the combined force of Dennis Lillee, Max Walker and Gary Gilmour, I got ahead of myself and was bowled by a nothing delivery from part-time seamer Greg Chappell.

Nevertheless, the experience of my consultation with Lee Saxon opened my eyes to the importance of mental well-being, and so when Bob Woolmer introduced psychometric testing and psychological profiling at Edgbaston fifteen years later I gave him my wholehearted support.

The positive energy that came from Saxon's techniques had brought a new self-confidence, and it was partly because of an enhanced sense of my own worth as a cricketer that I was so disappointed that I seemed to have been overlooked by Kerry Packer's organisation.

What's more, unlike most of the cricketing world, I felt sympathy for Kerry, particularly when the background to his going rogue and setting up WSC became public knowledge. As chairman of the Channel 9 television company, he had led the bid for the rights to cover Australia's home Test matches, and although his company had come first in the bidding process, the contract had been awarded without explanation or justification to Channel 7, who had been hand in glove with the Australian cricket authorities for many years. It was only after a subsequent failed attempt to get the decision reviewed independently that Kerry Packer embarked on his enterprising mission, and I couldn't help but admire his determination and tenacity in challenging an entrenched establishment that was, at the time, seemingly resistant to any form of change.

The hope that I might yet be approached to join WSC received a boost in late May when it was announced that Kerry Packer's aim was to sign up to fifty-one players in total. However, as more and more of the great West Indies side were reported to have signed, or to be about to sign contracts, it seemed that places were running out fast, and with the Ashes Tests not beginning until July, the only chance I had left to showcase my talents against the world's best was the one-day series against Australia in early June.

Of the four centuries that I scored in my 18 ODI appearances, the hundred at the Oval against Australia on 6 June was by far the best and the most significant. It was after this match that Greigy finally approached me. 'That was a wonderful innings out there today, Dennis,' he said. 'You really seem to enjoy one-day cricket.'

'I certainly do,' I replied. 'I love the freedom and the sense of adventure.'

'Well,' he said. 'If you fancy a bit of adventure, you might be interested in meeting Kerry Packer. He's in London as it happens and he wants to meet you.'

A few days later I found myself in a luxurious private suite in the Dorchester Hotel sitting opposite Kerry Packer and Richie Benaud, whose presence I found reassuring. As a commentator he had always talked of my batting in positive terms, and when we met socially he had appeared to take a genuine interest in me and my career. It was Kerry Packer, however, who spoke first: 'I watched your innings at the Oval the other day on the television,' he said. 'I was impressed.'

'We want you to offer you a contract to join us,' added Richie Benaud.

They then proceeded to take me through their plans, explaining that there would be an Australian XI, a West Indies XI and a World XI playing against each other, primarily at night and under floodlights. The salary on offer for six months was the equivalent in today's money of around £80,000, which was far more than my total annual earnings for Warwickshire and England including Test matches and winter tours. In addition, Kerry Packer made it clear that my family would be welcome to join me – all expenses paid for the entire six-month period.

At the age of 34, I had already started to think about life after cricket, and about how to ensure financial security for the family. Although my benefit in 1975 had raised a tax-free total of £35,000, which was well above par for the time, it was nowhere enough to provide a decent pension. Indeed, I still had another thirty-one working years before retirement. What's more, there was a new generation of talented cricketers emerging for England and Warwickshire, and I knew that it was only a matter of time before I would be surplus to requirements.

What I also knew, however, was that anyone who signed a contract with WSC would be unpopular with the hierarchies in every single cricket-playing nation. Closer to home, there were already leading figures at the Test and County Cricket Board and Warwickshire County Cricket Club who were calling for action to be taken to prevent more players from defecting to the 'rebel camp'.

In choosing whether to sign up with Kerry Packer or not, I had to balance the potential sacrifice of what was left of my playing career with England and Warwickshire against a seemingly speculative initiative that was untried, untested and unpopular. And yet within seconds of the offer of a contract being made I had made up my mind.

'I'd like to accept your offer,' I said, when Kerry Packer had finished outlining the terms and conditions under which I would be employed.

'Are you sure you don't want to sleep on it?' he replied.

'There's no pressure for you to sign here and now,' added Richie Benaud. 'You can go home and think about it if you like.'

I didn't see any need to think about it, and less than an hour and a half after arriving, I left the Dorchester with a copy of my WSC contract duly signed and dated. I had a real spring in my step, and absolutely no regrets about the decision I had made. It seemed to me that, given the very nature of professional sport, my future prospects as a Test player were no more certain, secure or calculable than as a member Kerry Packer's new organisation. In actual fact, of course, I was proved right within just four weeks: after successive failures in the first two matches of the Ashes series, I was dropped, having played my last Test for England.

Although I left the Dorchester with no regrets, the situation changed dramatically when I rang Jill to tell her the wonderfully exciting news. When I had finished explaining the terms of the contract, there was an icy pause before she responded: 'You didn't think to discuss it with me first?'

'It was too good an opportunity to miss,' I replied.

'And they insisted on you signing there and then, did they?'

'Well, no – er – no – not exactly,' I said, with ever increasing hesitancy.

'They either did or they didn't, Dennis.'

Although it didn't take Jill long to forgive me and to become as excited as I was at the prospect of a new adventure in our lives, she left me in no doubt at all about the importance of consultation, discussion and collaborative decision-making. It was a lesson that was to stand me in good stead in a number of critical situations in future years, particularly in my role as chief executive at Edgbaston.

Meanwhile, however, the International Cricket Council declared all-out war on Kerry Packer. At a meeting held in the last week of July they passed a resolution banning anyone who had joined WSC from Test cricket. The Test and County Cricket Board swiftly followed suit but went a step further, introducing an additional two-year ban on WSC cricketers playing county cricket.

While all of us who had signed for Packer realised that there were likely to be consequences of some sort, we were nonetheless shocked at the extent of the measures taken by the ICC and the establishment at Lord's. Moreover, having grown up in a deferential era when there was unquestioned acceptance of the authority of Lord's on all cricketing matters, I assumed that, with the ban having been announced, my conventional career in the game was done and dusted. Kerry Packer, however, had other ideas. He applied for an injunction and damages in the High Court against the International Cricket Conference (ICC) and Test and County Cricket Board (TCCB).

The court hearing began on 26 September, and although all of the fifty-one cricketers who had signed for WSC were affected by the ICC and TCCB bans, Kerry Packer's lawyers decided to fight the case on behalf of three individual plaintiffs: Tony Greig, John Snow and Mike Procter. Their reasoning was that any ruling given in favour of these three would also apply to the rest of us.

After thirty-one days, during which countless witnesses were called by both sides, Justice Slade gave his judgement in a summary that occupied 221 pages of foolscap and took five and a half hours to deliver. Ruling in favour of the three plaintiffs, the judge argued that the ICC and TCCB resolutions banning players from both international and county cricket were illegal as they represented an 'unreasonable restraint of trade'. He also found that the cricket authorities had acted improperly in seeking to force the plaintiffs to break their legally binding contracts with WSC.

Justice Slade's ruling was a hugely significant moment for the development and future direction of world cricket. It exposed the autocratic governance of the game and ended its monopoly of control, thus making possible various subsequent initiatives such as the highly successful Indian Premier League. The ruling also empowered all professional cricketers in demonstrating very clearly that they had rights and that their employer was not above the law of the land. Indeed, I believe that the emergence during the late 1970s of the Professional Cricketers' Association as a force to be reckoned with is no coincidence.

I am not naive enough to believe that Kerry Packer fought the court case and invested in WSC out of a philanthropic desire to better the lot of downtrodden cricketers. He was, first and foremost, a businessman intent on generating a handsome profit for himself and his shareholders. Nevertheless, whether it was by design or not, I believe that he initiated a whole range of changes that were long overdue, and without which the game might not have survived.

With its spirit of revolution and reform, the 1960s had been the decade of change. Most areas of society, including technology, popular culture, politics and education, had all undergone radical development to the point of transformation. Cricket, however, in its resistance to change had started to look increasingly out of step with the times. Apart from the reluctant introduction of one-day competitions, there had been no fundamental overhaul in the structural organisation or in the packaging and marketing of the game for almost a century.

That is not to say that the reforms and changes that Packer introduced were an instant success, nor that all of his innovations went according to plan. The main problem he faced, for example, was finding grounds in Australia that were big enough to accommodate the large crowds that his business model depended on, and which also offered wickets good enough to enable the world's best fast bowlers to deliver the ball at 90 miles per hour without killing the batsmen.

Not surprisingly, the Australian Cricket Board had used its influence to stop affiliated cricket associations and clubs from allowing a competitive organisation to use their grounds. Packer's solution was to lease VFL Park, Melbourne; Gloucester Park, Perth; and Moore Park in Sydney as his main venues. None of these places even remotely resembled a cricket ground, having been used for Australian rules football, horse racing and Sydney's annual agricultural show respectively.

Then, much to the annoyance of the Australian Cricket Board, who believed it would be impossible to make such venues fit for Test-match cricket, Kerry Packer wooed away one of their own – John Maley, who was the curator at the Gabba in Brisbane. In no time John had devised a plan to use hothouses in which to grow new pitches which were laid inside wicket-length metal trays. These could then be lowered by cranes into shallow trenches at each of the venues.

Although it was a brilliant idea, it had to be amended when the first crane sank into the ground at VFL Park, Melbourne, because of the weight of the tray it was lifting. Never one to be defeated by anything, however, Kerry Packer then hired a huge hovercraft to carry the pitch across the outfield to its destination in the middle of the field.

While the development of these portable installations was a logistical triumph, it was not an innovation that would have any long-term influence on the game. Like most new cricket pitches, John Maley's hothouse wickets behaved less predictably than more established surfaces which have matured and been carefully prepared over a number of seasons. Indeed, serious questions were asked about their safety when David Hookes was felled by a crushing bouncer from Andy Roberts that broke his jaw. This made everyone all the more aware that, in a competition dominated by the superquicks, there were likely to be more serious injuries unless something was done.

Since the 1974/75 Ashes series I had been looking for something that would provide protection against 90mph bouncers and, in preparation for joining WSC, I had gone to a motorcycle helmet manufacturer in Birmingham, who came up with a product that was lighter than the traditional fibreglass headgear. It also had a visor strong enough to withstand a shotgun blast at 10 yards.

Unlike the stylish design of modern helmets, my prototype was an ugly affair that looked a bit like a chamber pot and, not surprisingly, it was greeted initially with derision by the crowds and more than a few of my fellow players. The injury to David Hookes, however, was a key turning point. Within weeks half a dozen more had arrived from Birmingham and were soon being used by an increasing number of WSC players.

There were teething problems with these prototype helmets that had to be addressed. The visor, for example, was heavy and opaque and not suited to playing under the floodlights of night cricket. The biggest issue, however, was the lack of ventilation, which also impeded hearing. As a result there were a number of run-outs caused by the fact that the batsmen simply couldn't hear each other calling. This was highlighted, in particular, by an incident involving Alan Knott.

It was during a one-day match at Gloucester Park, Perth, between the WSC Australian XI and the WSC World XI. Knotty was batting with Imran Khan, who called him for a quick single and immediately changed his mind. In spite of Imran yelling 'go back, go back' at the top of his voice, Knotty kept coming and was duly run out by half the length of the pitch. On his way off the field, as had become customary in WSC, Knotty was joined by the Channel 9 television interviewer, together with microphone and cameraman. 'Bad luck, Knotty,' said the interviewer. 'I guess you didn't hear Imran's call.'

'I'm sorry,' replied Knotty, starting to unstrap his headgear. 'Can you say that again. I can't hear what you're saying with this helmet on.'

The ventilation and sound issues were soon addressed and, by the end of the second season of WSC, the majority of our players were wearing helmets, not simply for protection but also for the confidence that they provided. This was perfectly illustrated when David Hookes returned from his horrific injury to play in a match between WSC Australia and WSC World XI in Melbourne. When he came out to bat, he was immediately bounced by Wayne Daniels. Wearing a newly acquired helmet, David hooked the ball high, wide and handsome into the crowd for a glorious 6 and stood grinning as the West Indies paceman muttered deadly oaths. The fact that David had been able to come out to bat after his injury, without a hint of fear or psychological uncertainty, was almost certainly due to the protection that his new helmet provided.

Cricket helmets may not have been Kerry Packer's idea, but their development was made possible because of his openness to new ideas and initiatives. In complete contrast to cricket's established authorities at the time, he was never confined by tradition, and nor did he have to operate within the committee structure that so often prevented organisations like the ICC and TCCB from taking radical decisions. In this regard, he was a visionary pioneer, and his introduction of limited-overs cricket played at night under floodlights with a white ball was, without doubt, the precursor to the T20 version of the game that is now so popular around the cricketing world.

He also gave the administrators at Lord's a lesson in how to promote and market the modern game. As a highly successful media tycoon, he knew that the commercial viability of his television coverage of WSC depended, in the final analysis, on generating big crowds at the matches. Initially, however, very few people paid to come and watch WSC matches and Kerry feared that the images of empty grounds without any atmosphere that were being broadcast by his Channel 9 company would have a detrimental impact on attracting the television advertising that was his major source of revenue.

One of the secrets to Packer's success, however, was the swiftness of his response to any problem or crisis. Within a matter of days, his marketing team came up with an advertising jingle with the simple but catchy lyrics of 'Come on Aussies, come on'. After a week of it being repeated over and over again on Channel 9, not only did the crowds flood in, but during the matches involving WSC Australia you could hear them chanting the jingle from the terraces.

From a personal point of view, my experience of WSC was mixed. As far as playing was concerned, I started well with runs against both the West Indies and Australia. It was, however, a real challenge as a batsman to stay in form, not least because, with over thirty players competing for places in the WSC World XI, the opportunities we had to bat in the middle were limited. I was by no means the only player affected, and Asif Iqbal, Zaheer Abbas, Eddie Barlow and Tony Greig also struggled to find their batting rhythm. On a social level, however, I had a wonderful time, mainly because Jill and the children were with me. In addition, we enjoyed the company of the other players and their families, many of whom were already good friends from playing together for England.

The longer-term legacy that I gained from WSC was an understanding of some of the qualities required to manage a successful organisation. In later years, as chief executive of Warwickshire, my single-minded determination to bring success to the club, on and off the field, was in many ways inspired by the indomitable tenacity that Kerry Packer demonstrated in setting up WSC against all the obstacles that were put in his way. The decisions that the Warwickshire committee and I made to engage Bob Woolmer as Warwickshire coach and to take on Brian Lara as our overseas player were also influenced by Packer's insistence that 'you only get the best results if you have the best ingredients'.

Meanwhile, at the end of the first winter away with WSC, I returned to England for the domestic season. Without any realistic prospect of a recall to the England side, my focus was on playing as well as I could for Warwickshire. What I hadn't banked on, however, was being 'sent to Coventry' by a significant number of my county teammates, who still regarded me as a traitor for having signed with the rebels. One of the exceptions was David Brown, with whom I had been friends for many years. It wasn't that he agreed with my decision to join Packer – far from it – he was vehemently opposed to the breakaway organisation and did his level best to convince me that I had made a mistake in joining them. While our differences over Packer undoubtedly put a strain on our relationship, it survived the test of time, and we are still good friends to this day.

In general, though, there was an awkward silence throughout the 1978 season whenever I walked into the dressing room. Because of this, I made up my mind to spend as much time away from there as I possibly could and the obvious sanctuary was to be out in the middle, batting. And what a blessed release it was! Every second that I was out at the wicket doing battle with the opposition, I didn't have to suffer the hostility of some of my own team. The result was that, for only the second time in my career, I reached the target of 2,000 runs in a season, scoring seven 100s and another eleven 50s along the way.

The antipathy towards me at Edgbaston was not only confined to the dressing room. My contract was due to expire at the end of the season, and in spite of the prolific number of runs I was scoring, I was informed towards the end of July by AC Smith, the secretary of Warwickshire, that the club would not be offering me new terms for the 1979 season. While the explanation given was that the club wanted to develop younger talent, it was perfectly clear that the real reason I was being sacked was because I had signed for Packer.

It was Jack Bannister, a former colleague at Warwickshire, who saved my career. Widely respected in the game, he had become a key figure in the running of the Professional Cricketers' Association, and his diplomatic skills had become increasingly evident in his representation of players affected by the Packer affair.

It was some weeks after my predicament with Warwickshire became public knowledge that Jack rang me to say that he had set up a meeting with AC Smith and the club chairman, Cyril Goodway, to try and resolve the situation. While I was very grateful for Jack's support, I had little or no confidence that he would be able to reverse a decision made by one of the most hard-line anti-Packer cricket committees in the country.

When we were all assembled in the secretary's office, it was Jack Bannister who opened the meeting with a question directed at AC Smith and Cyril Goodman. 'If Kerry Packer and the Australian Cricket Board signed a peace agreement, that would then be endorsed by the ICC and TCCB, would Warwickshire agree to give Dennis a new contract?'

'I think we could go along with that,' said AC, before turning to Cyril Goodman. 'Don't you agree, Chairman?'

Much to my surprise and delight, the meeting ended with an undertaking from AC and Cyril Goodway that they would support a recommendation to the committee that I would get a new contract to enable me to continue my playing career with the club.

What I hadn't appreciated, of course, is that Jack had been tipped the wink about secret negotiations between Packer and the cricketing authorities that were nearing conclusion. His source was none other than Richie Benaud, who was one of Kerry Packer's closest and most trusted confidants.

Jack and Richie had been very good friends for many years and shared a passion for horse racing. Every Saturday morning, in spite of the time difference between England and Australia, they phoned each other to discuss the day's racing programme and which horses they were going to bet on.

It was during one of these conversations that Benaud had told Jack about the negotiations taking place. He had also informed him that the only thing standing in the way of the peace treaty being signed was Kerry Packer's insistence that an end be put to what he believed was a continuing witch hunt against his players. As far as Kerry was concerned, my sacking by Warwickshire was a case in point.

Unknown to me, Jack had phoned AC Smith prior to setting up our meeting and shared Richie Benaud's news. Thus, when I walked into the room for the meeting, the decision to reverse my sacking was a foregone conclusion. It was in everyone's interests to bring the war between WSC and the establishment to an end, and Warwickshire could not be seen as the only organisation blocking the way of peace.

13

Mutineer, Management, Motivation and Mentoring

In many ways the agreement that was finally reached in the summer of 1979 between Kerry Packer and the Australian Cricket Board was a truce in name only. There was considerable relief in Australia that Packer had agreed to bring an end to the WSC tournaments; they had taken crowds and revenue away from official Test matches. Nevertheless, there were influential members of the ICC and TCCB who felt deep resentment at the deal that Packer had managed to negotiate. Not only did the settlement give his television company the exclusive rights to broadcast Australian cricket, but he also got a ten-year deal to promote and market the game Down Under.

It took a long time for everyone to forgive and forget the deep divisions that had been opened up by the Packer dispute, and the Warwickshire dressing room was no exception. The pregnant pauses in conversation when I walked into the room continued long into the 1980 season. There were some players who took even longer to let bygones be bygones and, inevitably I suppose, there are one or two who never have.

The new contract that I had signed with Warwickshire, after my sacking had been rescinded, committed me to the club to the end of the 1982 season, after which I envisaged retiring from the game. My plan, in the meantime, was to use every opportunity to prepare for the future, and because I was confident that I would not be going away on England tours for four months at a time, I hoped to use the winters to develop a post-cricket career.

It was something of a surprise, therefore, when I was approached towards the end of the 1981 season by a senior England player: 'I've been asked to sound you out, Dennis,' he said. 'You're obviously in good form; you've been scoring a lot of runs for Warwickshire and the powers-that-be wondered if you'd be interested in coming to India this winter. You've got a good record against the spinners.'

'I'm flattered to be asked,' I replied, 'but I've toured India twice and I think you'd be better off looking for someone else – someone younger – building for the future.'

It may seem strange, having spent so much of my career stubbornly focused on getting into the England side, that I should turn down such an opportunity. The offer was, in many ways, very tempting; it would have given me the chance to put the disappointment of low scores in my last two Tests against Australia behind me, and end my international career on a high note. In truth, though, I knew that my heart wouldn't be in yet another comeback. The years that I had spent striving for success at the highest level had taken their psychological toll. The spark of enthusiasm for international cricket had gone out, and it would have been wrong not to be honest about that.

A few months after this, however, I was at home in Birmingham when the phone rang. Whoever it was on the other end of the line had a heavily guttural South African accent: 'Is that Dennis Amiss?' he asked. 'It's Ali Bacher here. I'm sorry about the crackling on the line. I'm ringing you from Johannesburg. I hope you can hear me, as I've got a proposition to put to you.'

After half an hour's conversation with the former South African captain, and getting Jill's approval, I accepted an invitation to take part in a four-week tour to South Africa beginning in March as part of an unofficial England team. During our discussion Ali had made it clear that total secrecy was essential and that neither the tour itinerary, nor the names of the England players involved, would be released to the press until our arrival in Johannesburg.

Ali Bacher's main coup had been to persuade Geoff Boycott to sign both as a player and as his main recruitment agent. And so, while my invitation came direct from Ali Bacher, Geoff Boycott, who was on the MCC tour to India, was busily recruiting as many of the other England players as he could. In fact, he proved to be a master of subterfuge, arranging a series of clandestine meetings. He even used codewords drawn from chess to conceal his machinations from the management. He was so successful as an undercover agent that he managed to sign up half the team without the captain, Keith Fletcher, finding out what was going on.

The reason for the intense secrecy was because of the political sensitivities surrounding South Africa. There hadn't been an official England cricket tour there since their government's refusal to allow Basil D'Oliveira's entry into the country as a member of the 1968 MCC touring party because of their apartheid laws. Rugby, athletics and football had all followed cricket's example, banning South Africa from competing at international level, and the anti-apartheid movement – set up by Peter Hain in 1970 to stop the Springbok rugby tour to England – had become increasingly vociferous and influential.

After fourteen years of imposed international isolation, interest in South Africa's domestic cricket competitions was rapidly waning. As a consequence, their cricket authorities had decided to follow Kerry Packer's example and organise Test-match-style cricket outside the jurisdiction of the ICC or TCCB.

With the financial backing of South African Breweries, they were able to pay members of the touring party more in a month than we could earn in three years as an England Test player. Not surprisingly, therefore, players like me, Geoff Boycott, Alan Knott and Derek Underwood, whose Test careers were either over or coming towards the end, jumped at the chance. Some of the younger players like John Emburey and Graham Gooch, who captained the side, decided to sign contracts because they saw it as an opportunity to ease the financial pressures that come with bringing up a young family on a professional cricketer's salary.

We all realised that the tour would be controversial and unpopular but none of us foresaw the full extent of the furore that followed the announcement of our arrival in South Africa. The British tabloids had a field day, with the *Daily Mirror* describing the team as 'Gooch's Dirty Dozen'. Cricket correspondents and political journalists vilified us, and there was even a heated debate about the tour in the House of Commons, during which the Labour MP Gerald Kaufmann claimed that we were mercenaries who had sold ourselves 'for blood-covered Krugerrands'.

Pressure grew on the TCCB to take decisive action and, after a four-hour emergency meeting at Lord's, they issued a three-year Test-match ban on every member of the team, arguing that we had 'deliberately and willfully ignored the TCCB's policy in respect of sporting connections with South Africa'. Although it wasn't a decision that would affect me, I felt great sympathy for the younger members of the team. Graham Gooch, for instance – still in his 20s – was about to be deprived of some of his prime years as a Test batsman.

Matters came to a head for me personally when the increasingly bellicose public reaction to the tour began to affect Jill and the children at home in England. There were newspaper reporters camped outside our house in Birmingham, and every time Jill either came or went, she had to run the gauntlet of hostile questions and flashing cameras. Worse still was the abuse that our 8-year-old son, Paul, had to endure from other children in the playground at school. Something had to be done, and within hours of discovering the full extent of the bullying, I had arranged for the whole family to join me in South Africa for the rest of the tour.

Although I was able to take steps to protect Jill and the children from the media hostility, there was very little I could do to protect myself when we got home from the tour. Along with Derek Underwood and Alan Knott, I was now labelled a 'double rebel' for having signed with Packer and gone on the South African tour. As a consequence, we were singled out for particular criticism, and all of us were treated with particular disdain and contempt on our return to England.

Almost forty years after the tour I still feel a sense of injustice at the way we were condemned. It seems to me that cricket was seen by politicians and the media as an easy and convenient way to establish their anti-apartheid credentials. There was no embargo on people travelling to and from South Africa for business or leisure; leading British companies had branches across the country, and there were precious few commercial or financial sanctions. Furthermore, numerous other sports, including golf, motor racing and tennis had no restrictions on players competing with, or against, South Africans.

The real irony was that cricket, which had become the central focus of the anti-apartheid movement, was the one and only sport in South Africa to have become fully integrated. In fact, the South African Cricket Union (SACU) had been formed in 1976 with the express purpose of administering the game on a 'multi-racial, meritocratic basis'. What's more, the ICC fact-finding group that toured the Republic two years before the rebel tour concluded that cricket had become open to players of all ethnicities. Indeed, the terms of the agreements we had signed were an illustration of the SACU's drive to make the game fully integrated, and, in addition to playing, we were all required to coach children from all the racial groups represented across the country.

From a cricketing point of view, the tour was decidedly mixed. As a team, we were outplayed by a highly competitive South African XI that included the world-class talents of Barry Richards, Graham Pollock and Mike Procter, all of whom were desperate to show world cricket what it had been missing for more than a decade. From a personal point of view, however, it could hardly have gone better; I scored four half-centuries, at an average of over 60, in the three unofficial Tests against a hostile attack led by Garth le Roux and Vincent van der Bijl.

It wasn't until I got back to England for the start of the 1982 season, however, that I began to appreciate just how much living through the controversy of Packer and the rebel tour had taken out of me. My skin itched all over, and I was covered in an unsightly and uncomfortable rash. In truth I was physically and emotionally exhausted, and as I drove into Edgbaston for the first day of pre-season training I had more or less accepted that, with my contract expiring at the end of the summer, this would be my final season as a professional cricketer. 'Perhaps it's time to move on,' I thought to myself. 'Time for a change; time for a new challenge.'

I had in fact started to reinvent myself as a businessman a couple of winters before, working for Roger Hamilton-Brown, whose son, Rory, went on to play successfully for Surrey and Sussex. Roger was the founder and chief executive of Officescape, a rapidly developing new company that had begun by specialising in office partitioning. He was a brilliant salesman who combined infectious enthusiasm with a magnetic personal charm and a wonderful sense of humour.

My role in the enterprise was to make new contacts wherever and whenever I could. It involved travelling hundreds of miles a week between our offices in Birmingham and London in search of new business. For someone who has always enjoyed meeting and engaging with new people it didn't feel like work, and I learned a lot about running a business from Roger and another colleague, Stuart Spires, who ran the Birmingham office. Both men were enterprising, hard working and full of ideas.

'The key is to make the little that we have got work for us to the absolute maximum,' Roger said to me the morning after we had landed our first big contract. This was a philosophy that I completely understood, as it had been the fundamental principle that had always underpinned my approach to batsmanship. I had known from the outset of my cricket career that there were players with more natural talent than me, and so I built my game on maximising the strengths that I did have.

Roger did exactly the same in developing Officescape. Once he had signed his first big contract with Dow Chemicals, and completed the development of a vast office space in a complex close to Heathrow airport, he used it to our maximum advantage. We took all our potential customers to view the newly developed area as an illustration of the quality of our workmanship and the scale of the developments we were capable of fulfilling.

Our combined efforts worked like a charm, and before long we had completed numerous lucrative contracts, including the development of offices for Citibank. We also expanded our range of services and in addition to the physical partitioning of office spaces, we began to offer a full design-and-build package which included space planning and interior design – all provided by our own in-house creative team.

The expansion of the firm also brought a promotion, and as I arrived at Edgbaston for the start of what I thought would be my last season as a professional cricketer, my plan was to return to Officescape in September as a director of the company. The very last thing on my mind was the thought that I might carry on for five more summers.

It was towards the end of the 1982 season that I started to have second thoughts about retiring from the game. David Brown, who had taken on the role of cricket manager at Warwickshire, approached me at the end of a day's play against Yorkshire at Headingley; I'd batted particularly well, falling just six short of a century in the second innings.

'You should have got a hundred today, Dennis,' he said.

'Don't rub it in,' I replied.

'Fair enough, but do you know how many first-class centuries that would have been?'

'No idea,' I replied.

'It would have been your 87th. You're on 86 at the moment.'

Now, I know there are lots of batsmen who will give you chapter and verse on every personal statistic imaginable; they know exactly how many runs they have scored in a season and can recite their batting average down to the last decimal point, but I was never one of them. Yes – I have always been totally focused on scoring runs, but counting them or keeping detailed records was not for me, and so I was genuinely amazed when David Brown told me I had that many centuries to my name.

But the conversation didn't end there. 'Why don't you commit to playing on for four or possibly five more seasons?' he said.

'I can't play on forever, David,' I replied. 'I'm 39 – I've done God knows how many seasons already. You've got some good young batters to bring on.'

'That's exactly why we want you to stay, Dennis: to bring on the young batsmen. Andy Lloyd, Asif Din, KD Smith – they've got a lot of promise – they're the future of the club – but they're young and inexperienced and they need guidance. Not in the nets but out there in the middle, where it counts, and that's why we want you to play on – to be out there with them, give them the benefit of all those twenty-four seasons. And you never know: you only need fourteen more tons to have 100 hundreds, to be up there with Geoff Boycott – you'd like that.'

'I'm not sure he would,' I added. And we laughed.

Having played together for over twenty years, David knew me as well as I knew myself, and he understood exactly what would spark up the dying embers of my cricketing ambitions. Had he focused solely on the fact that, by playing on, I stood the chance of getting a 100 first-class hundreds, I doubt very much that I would have changed my mind. The fact that I had no idea how many centuries I'd already scored indicates that records had never been that important to me. Had he suggested that I continue simply to help with the development of Warwickshire's young batsmen, I would have been equally unpersuaded. As my career after playing demonstrates, I had no particular aptitude or appetite for becoming a coach.

It was the combination of the two goals that appealed to me, and the more I thought about it, the more I saw that they were linked. My ambition to succeed as a batsman had been inspired by the supreme batting skills of Denis Compton, Ken Barrington, Ted Dexter and Tom Graveney. Had they settled for less than they were capable of achieving, my own sights would have been lowered.

What kept going through my mind following the conversation with David Brown was the thought that if I could give to Warwickshire's young batting triumvirate – Asif Din, Andy Lloyd and KD Smith – just a touch of the same inspiration and ambition that Compton, Barrington, Dexter and Graveney had given me, I could play on with a renewed sense of purpose and fulfilment. I also knew that in spite of advancing years, if I was to have anywhere near the influence on the trio that my heroes had on me, I would need to bat to the very best of my ability, and in so doing I would, in all likelihood, reach the target of 100 first-class hundreds that David Brown had set for me.

The reality of my relationship with Asif, Andy and KD over the next few seasons, however, was that I learned every bit as much from them as I hope they learned from me. I didn't try to play the role of coach, nor seek to tamper with their techniques; they were good players who had their own methods that worked well for them. Nor was our relationship based on seniority; it was the 1980s and the hierarchical structure that had been in place when I joined the club in 1958 was long gone. We saw ourselves as teammates and fellow practitioners, and my role was simply to share what I knew about the art of batsmanship.

The only difference between us was that I had played longer and enjoyed many more successes and disappointments than the three of them put together. With this in mind, I did what I could to relieve the pressure on them; I would, for example, ensure that I faced the majority of deliveries from a bowler who was causing them particular problems. I also chatted to them between overs when things were getting tense; it often didn't matter what was said, it was the calm and reassuring tone of voice that was important. After all, there is nothing more guaranteed to generate anxiety than the fear-filled cries of 'don't panic, don't panic' that were the hallmark of Clive Dunn's highly strung Corporal Jones in *Dad's Army*.

While I may have helped them with the mental side of their games, there is no doubt that they covered for the physical deficiencies in mine. This was particularly evident during a match against Derbyshire at Derby. Having opened the innings, I found myself nursing what felt like a pulled muscle after just a couple of overs at the crease. As a consequence I was unable to run, and Geoff Miller, the Derbyshire skipper, kindly agreed to allow me to have assistance. Thus it was that Asif, Andy and KD, who had all got out for low scores, came out in turn to act as my runner as I made my way to a century.

As our second innings approached, my muscle strain seemed to have eased off, and so I felt able to bat again. All was going well until I attempted a quick single and felt that telltale tightening in the calf for the second time in three days. Once again Asif, Andy and KD were summoned in turn to act as my runner as I limped on to my second century of the match.

Running the runs for another batsman is hard enough, particularly when you have failed to post a score yourself. It must have been especially galling for poor Andy Lloyd; he had been run out cheaply in both innings while batting with me. I dread to think what curses he was uttering under his breath as he scampered up and down the wicket.

In many ways those final years with Warwickshire were the happiest and most relaxed of my playing career. I no longer felt that I had anything to prove as a player but I was, nonetheless, driven to perform as well as I possibly could by a professional pride that remained undiminished. In this respect my one real fear was to outstay my welcome and become one of those players who cannot accept that their time is up because they have nothing else in their lives to fall back on.

It was this thought that kept going through my mind as the 1986 season drew to its close. I had scored my hundredth first-class century against Lancashire at the end of July. I had done what I could to encourage and support the younger players' development, and I had been delighted at Andy Lloyd's inclusion in the England side two seasons earlier.

'I'm 43 years old,' I said to myself. 'I can't play on forever.'

And yet, at the back of my mind, there was a niggling thought that wouldn't go away. 'That hundred against Lancashire was a "gimme". Clive Lloyd handed it to you on a plate. It may be in the record books, but it doesn't count, and if you're honest, Dennis, you'll admit it; you haven't got 100 first-class hundreds – not really – you've got ninety-nine. You're one short of the target. Are you happy with that? Are you going to retire pretending you're a member of that exclusive club: Bradman, Cowdrey, Graveney, Ames, Hobbs and all the other greats? 'Cos that's all it will be – one big pretence.'

The big question was what would the club feel about me playing on for one more season. Norman Gifford had joined us from

Worcestershire as captain the previous season and, knowing that Giff would always give me a straight answer, I asked him whether he still wanted me in the side.

'I'd be delighted, Dennis,' he replied. 'You got four hundreds this season; only Brian McMillan scored more runs than you. Don't give up if you don't feel ready – not just because of your age. I'm three years older than you and I'm not retiring, not while I'm still taking wickets. As long as you keep scoring runs you'll be one of the first names on the team sheet.'

Thus it was that when the Warwickshire squad assembled at Edgbaston on a freezing cold early spring morning, Monday, 6 April 1987 – the day before my 44th birthday – I changed into my tracksuit ready to embark on the twenty-ninth and final season of my long playing career.

The pre-season dressing-room banter was little changed from previous seasons: catching up on cricketing gossip, comparing winter jobs and discussing the schedule for the coming season: 'Why do we always play Kent at Tunbridge Wells?'; 'Hasn't anyone at Lord's ever seen a map of the UK? Hove to Scarborough! That's ridiculous!'; 'I'm not looking forward to the Oval – not if they leave all the grass on like last season – Sylvester Clarke was lethal; hey Alvin – remember that ball he bowled that nearly killed you?'

It was a strange feeling sitting there in the midst of all these light-hearted exchanges, realising that this was the beginning of the end for me as a professional cricketer. I couldn't help but reflect on the nerves and apprehension I had felt as a 15-year-old when I'd first joined the staff. It had taken me a long time to feel that I really belonged at Edgbaston and now, twenty-nine years on, I had a powerful realisation that in just a few months I would cease to be part of what had become my extended family.

In the meantime, however, I had one more task to fulfil, and on 29 July 1986 at Worcester, almost exactly a year on from my 'official' 100th first-class century against Lancashire, I set aside all doubts about the legitimacy of the achievement. There were no trumpets or fanfares to mark this unofficial but very personal moment, and yet, as I sat in the dressing room at New Road, run out for 123 off the last ball of our innings, I knew that I had no more unfinished business as a player.

By the time I scored the final first-class hundred of my career against Leicestershire at Hinkley, I had already announced my retirement from the game, and this time I was entirely happy with the decision. It wasn't just that I felt fulfilled, nor that I had the prospect of an exciting new career ahead of me; the reason that I felt no regrets at leaving my playing days behind was that the decision had been entirely mine – I had been one of the very lucky players who choose the time that they move on.

Over the twenty-nine seasons during which I had been a professional cricketer, I had seen too many teammates leave the game disappointed and resentful at the manner and timing of their departure. Whether they had left because of injury, loss of form or lack of ability, the common denominator was that none of them had been in control of events. It was because of this that, when I became CEO at Warwickshire, I always did my utmost to encourage the younger players, in particular, to prepare for life after cricket at the earliest possible stage. While planning for a second career doesn't guarantee protection against the variables that bring an end to playing, it does open up opportunities and choices for the next stage in life.

At the end of my final season as a player, Warwickshire did me proud. There was a dinner held in my honour at Edgbaston attended by representatives from every first-class county, the TCCB, MCC and the Professional Cricketers' Association. Jack Bannister and David Graveney gave speeches that were embarrassingly fulsome about my contribution to the game. In return, I was able to use the opportunity to thank everyone who had helped me along the way – from the coaching and advice of Tiger Smith and Tom Dollery in the early years, to the wise management and captaincy of David Brown and Norman Gifford in more recent times.

It was a humbling and emotional night but, perhaps ironically, it seemed more like a rapprochement than a farewell, and I felt that the cricketing establishment was officially accepting the 'double rebel' back into the fold.

My full redemption was confirmed almost immediately after my retirement when I accepted Warwickshire's invitation to become chairman of their cricket committee; this was to lead in turn to my appointment in 1994 as chief executive of the club. In the meantime, however, I devoted my working life to a new business. The title of my job was Acquisitions Director for Hodgson Holdings, who ran a chain of funeral homes across the country, and my role was the purchase and rationalisation of small, local undertakers.

Inevitably, I suppose, the jokes and quips from old friends about the nature of my employer's business were endless: 'I'll bet you're *dead* excited about your new job Dennis'; 'Rationalising funeral homes must be quite an *undertaking!*'; 'You've been searching for the Ashes all your career, Dennis, and now you have finally found them.'

It was all in good fun and I didn't mind at all, not least because the job enabled me to develop my business acumen through working in a highly competitive market for a rapidly expanding company with a national profile. On one occasion, for instance, I had the opportunity to travel to America with Howard Hodgson, who had inherited the company from his father and become the leading pioneer in the rationalisation of the funeral business structure in the UK. Not content with this, however, his mission in crossing the Atlantic was to take over one of the USA's leading funeral directors, and the trip proved a fascinating insight into high-level business negotiations.

The meeting opened with the effervescent Howard delivering his lengthy sales pitch about the benefits of the Hodgson Holdings rationalisation exercise, based on the exceptionally cost-efficient model of six funeral homes sharing one set of cars and one team of personnel. It was only in his conclusion that Howard revealed to the management team of the American company that his reason for setting up the meeting was that he wanted to buy the American company out.

'Wow!' said the American CEO when Howard had finished. 'That was some spiel! You say you wanna buy us out; well, let me tell you straight, Howard, we wanna buy you out.'

Although we came home from the trip empty-handed, it made me realise that aspiration is as important to the success of a business organisation as it is to a sporting individual. In the words of the great Bill Shankley: 'If you aim for the sky, you'll reach the ceiling; if you aim for the ceiling, you'll stay on the floor.' And it was precisely this philosophy that became my mantra when, eventually, I took over from David Heath as chief executive of Warwickshire County Cricket Club.

14

Leadership, Lara and Laurels

By the beginning of the 1990s there was an emerging recognition throughout cricket that the management of the professional game was no longer fit for purpose. With falling attendances at matches and declining membership, county cricket clubs, in particular, were all too aware of the need to be more businesslike. One of the key developments that took place, as a consequence, was the phasing out of the role of county cricket club secretary in favour of a newly created position of chief executive officer. It was, however, more than just a change in title, and the main emphasis in the redefined job specification was on commercial acumen as opposed to administrative ability or, indeed, a knowledge of cricket.

As more and more counties appointed candidates from corporate business or industry as CEOs, it seemed that the days of former players like Les Ames, Donald Carr or AC Smith becoming the senior administrators of county cricket clubs were over.

Thus, when Warwickshire announced that the post of CEO at Edgbaston would become vacant in January 1994, following David Heath's retirement, I knew, if I applied, I wouldn't be a shoo-in. It wasn't that I didn't have the business experience required for the job; for the seven years since my retirement as a player I had sat on the board as an executive director of Hodgson Holdings and played a significant role in its development as a highly successful public company.

Nonetheless, I knew that however successful I might have been in my business career, there were members of the appointment panel who would always see me, first and foremost, as a cricketer. As well as that, the fact that I had retained a close involvement with the club as chairman of the cricket committee was something of a double-edged sword. While it meant that I had an intimate knowledge of the club and its personnel, there was a strong argument that an outsider was needed to introduce the changes necessary for success on and off the field.

As anticipated, the majority of the candidates and, indeed, the eventual shortlist, had strong commercial backgrounds, and so it was something of a surprise that the final choice was between two ex-players: me and Jim Cumbes, who had played first-class cricket for four counties, including Warwickshire. After retiring as a player he had been both popular and successful as the marketing manager at Edgbaston before moving on to the Oval in a similar capacity.

As I discovered later from a member of the appointment panel, although the decision went in my favour it was a very close-run thing; the success that Jim Cumbes had enjoyed in his role at the Oval, together with his engaging charm and charisma, made him a very strong candidate, and I was delighted that just a few weeks after his disappointment at Edgbaston he landed the job as Lancashire's CEO at Old Trafford.

A few weeks later, on a cold January morning in 1994, I drove into the ground at Edgbaston and parked my car for the first time in the space marked 'Reserved for The Chief Executive Officer'. As I sat for a few moments contemplating the challenge ahead of me, I couldn't help but remember the 15-year-old boy who had arrived at the ground, thirty-six years previously, full of nervous excitement and apprehension on his first day as a professional cricketer.

I thought, too, of Leslie Deakins, Warwickshire's secretary, who had offered me my first contract back in 1958. He had served the club for almost fifty years, overseeing the development of the ground as a modern Test-match stadium, and the building of two County Championship-winning sides. He was a man for whom I always had the greatest respect, and as I took my place behind the desk in what had been his office, I vowed to myself that I would do my utmost to build on his legacy.

In recent years Warwickshire's fortunes had slipped from the more successful era of the 1970s. It was something that I was very conscious of during my six years as chairman of the cricket committee. Indeed, there were times when I felt frustrated that the club's ambitions seemed to be constrained by history. Having only won the County Championship three times in over 100 years, mid-table finishes had gradually become the expectation.

My experience of playing for Kerry Packer and of working in two forward-thinking businesses had taught me that success is dependent on creating a culture of aspiration. I also knew that the foundations for high achievement could only be laid by recruiting the right people to key positions.

The first significant step in this context was the signing of Dermot Reeve in 1988. I had only been chairman of cricket for a few months, but the moment the cricket committee and I heard that he was unsettled at Sussex because of a lack of opportunity, we knew he was what was needed at Edgbaston. Although by no means the most talented all-rounder in the country, he was undoubtedly the most enthusiastic and wholehearted young cricketer I had seen in a long time. Highly competitive and outspoken, he made no secret of his ambition to play at the highest level. He was also well known for introducing innovation and a spirit of adventure into his play, and everyone on the cricket committee was convinced that he would be a dynamic influence in the Warwickshire dressing room. What's more, at 25 years old and driven by a deep need to prove himself, his game could only improve with a consequent impact on the team's fortunes. And so it proved, as we climbed from 15th in the County Championship in 1987 to 5th in Dermot's first season with the club. The positive influence that he had on the side was such that he was the natural successor as captain when Andy Lloyd decided to step down from the post at the end of the 1992 season.

In recruiting Dermot Reeve we had put the first piece of the jigsaw in place, but, as everyone knows, the most important next step is to connect all the outer edge and corner sections of the puzzle. In this context, it was the appointment of Bob Woolmer as coach in 1991 that provided us with the overall framework within which all the other constituent parts started to make sense.

I had known Bob as a cricketing colleague for England, and as a fellow member of WSC and the rebel tour to South Africa in 1982. Not only was he a close personal friend, but I also regarded him as the best and most innovative young coach in the world. He had already made his mark in South Africa as a pioneer in promoting cricket and raising playing standards among what was then known as the 'coloured' community. His success in developing players at Avendale Cricket Club in Cape Town had led to his appointment in 1987 as the coach at his former county, Kent, just three years after his retirement as a player.

In actual fact, I had played a significant role in his return to Canterbury. Chris Cowdrey, who was skipper of the Hoppers, was very keen to have Bob as their new coach and wanted to persuade the powers-that-be that he was the man for the job. It was because of this that – during a winter cricket cruise, six months before the 1987 season was due to begin – I was primed by Chris to dine with EW (Jim) Swanton, who was a member of the Kent committee. Not surprisingly, the subject of Kent's search for a new coach came up during the meal: 'Tell me, Dennis, old boy,' said EW in his plummy, aristocratic accent, 'what do you think of Bob Woolmer as a coach?'

'He's excellent, Jim,' I replied. 'In fact, I'd go so far as to say he's the best around.'

EW was clearly impressed, and within no more than a few days after our return from the cruise, Bob had signed a three-year contract with Kent.

Returning to his old club as coach so soon after finishing as a player was never going to be easy, and so, on discovering that he was not entirely happy at Canterbury, I persuaded the other members of the cricket committee to bring him to Edgbaston for the start of the 1991 season.

His impact on the side was instant, and the younger players in particular responded to his infectious enthusiasm. More than that, however, he proved to be a brilliant technical coach. No less a judge than Jason Ratcliffe, who had been on the playing staff for three years before Bob's arrival, maintains to this day that he was 'the one coach who really made a difference in improving players' performances on the field. He was way ahead of his time in introducing things like psychometric analysis in order to understand us all as individuals.'

Bob was, indeed, a master of innovation and never afraid to experiment with new ideas and techniques; the reverse sweep and the numerous varieties of well-disguised slower balls – standard in today's one-day competitions – were introduced by him at Warwickshire in the early 1990s, and although some of our more traditional supporters were horrified at this departure from the MCC coaching manual, the improvement in results was there for all to see. We finished runners-up in the Championship in 1991 – Bob's first season at the club – and then won the NatWest Trophy two years later. What pleased me most, however, was the ambition that Bob brought to the club. As a player, he had been part of a Kent side that had carried all before it in the 1970s, and he instilled the same winning mentality throughout the Warwickshire playing squad.

While he emphasised the need for players to take individual responsibility, he also expected them to put the overall interests of the team above their personal ambitions. In this context, whenever anything went wrong, on or off the field of play, he was adamant that the whole team went out together the same evening to discuss the issue over dinner. It didn't matter what plans individuals might have made, he was insistent that they all attend. As a result, things were never left to fester. What's more, a culture of openness developed such that players were able to express themselves freely but also understood the importance of listening to each other.

The third key decision that I was involved in as chairman of the cricket committee was the appointment in 1993 of Steve Rouse as head groundsman. Following his retirement as a player in 1983, the former left-arm seamer had set up a successful business working as a sports ground maintenance contractor. It wasn't long before he had responsibility for several of the club grounds where our 2nd XI played home fixtures. We were so impressed by the quality of the wickets he prepared that we decided to appoint him to the post at Edgbaston.

Not surprisingly, the former fast bowler's main mission on arrival at Edgbaston was to prepare wickets that combined pace and bounce; hour after hour, throughout his first year at the club, he drove the heavy roller up and down the square until the surface shone like polished glass. It wasn't until the West Indian fast bowler Curtly Ambrose ran in to bowl the first ball of the 1995 Test match at Edgbaston that we all realised that Steve might have overdone the rolling just a little. The ball thudded into the ground, halfway down the pitch, and took off, flying over the batsman and wicketkeeper before crashing, one bounce, into the sight screen.

England's batsmen were bowled out cheaply in both innings and the match was over by lunchtime on the third day – with the consequent loss of revenue from the fourth and fifth days' play. We only managed to appease the Saturday crowd, who had only seen half a day's play, by allowing them to have picnics on the outfield when the game was finished.

Thereafter, Steve moderated his approach and we were soon playing on wickets that produced exactly what was needed: entertaining cricket and results. Indeed, we only ever had one more issue as far as the quality of pitches at Edgbaston was concerned. It was the First Test of the 1997 series against Australia, and the moment I saw the wicket on the morning of the match I knew we could be in for trouble. It looked terrible, mottled in colour and already showing signs of cracking.

With Australia all out for 118 in their first innings, I feared that – once again – the game would not last three days. Fortunately for the future of Test cricket at Edgbaston, the wicket was tamed by heavy rain, the match lasted four days and brought in record gate receipts of £1,588,593. Nonetheless, we received an official letter from AC Smith – by then chief executive of the TCCB – informing us 'with regret' that if the pitches at Edgbaston did not improve then the board would consider taking 'Test Match cricket away from Edgbaston'.

The problem with the pitch had nothing to with Steve Rouse's excellent and thorough preparations; the cracking of the surface had been caused by our controversial new pitch covering. Known locally as the 'Brumbrella', the massive covers were highly effective in protecting the square from rainfall, but also prevented natural moisture and nutrients from getting into the soil; it was this that had caused the cracking and plating on the square. Getting rid of them was a tough decision as they had saved many days' play in county cricket, Test matches and ODIs from being called off because of a waterlogged pitch. In the end, however, we couldn't jeopardise Test cricket at Edgbaston and the 'Brumbrella' had to go.

It wasn't until I took up my post as CEO that I was able to put the final piece of the Warwickshire jigsaw in place. Allan Donald, our fast-bowling overseas player, was selected as a member of the South African side touring England during the 1994 season. As a result he was unavailable to play for Warwickshire that summer. On Dermot Reeve's advice, we signed Manoj Prabhakar on a one-year contract as Allan's overseas replacement. Regarded as the best all-rounder in the world at the time, we hoped that Manoj would provide the touch of something special that would bring us the Championship we hadn't won for over twenty years.

Six weeks before Manoj was due to arrive at Edgbaston for pre-season training, I got the news that he had suffered an ankle injury during a ODI match against Sri Lanka and would be out of action for a significant part of the summer. I immediately decided to contact MJK Smith, the chairman of Warwickshire. He was away in the Caribbean as manager of the England tour, but I eventually got through to him on the telephone. 'I think we should try and settle with Prabhakar's agent and find a replacement overseas player for the summer,' I said. 'The trouble is, it's very late in the day.'

'Who do you want to replace him?' he asked.

'I've discussed it with the cricket committee and we think Brian Lara's the right man. He seems to get runs every time he goes to the wicket against England.'

'He's certainly impressed me on this tour,' he said. 'I rate him highly.'

'Yes, but would he want to join us?' I asked.

'I don't know,' said MJK, 'but we're playing against him again tomorrow so I can find out.'

Having confirmed that he was available and willing to join us for a season, Brian Lara agreed to become our overseas player at a salary of £40,000 for the season. Luck was undoubtedly on our side as he signed the contract on 15 April, the day before the Test match in Antigua was due to begin. Had we waited another day to get his signature there is no way we could have afforded to engage him. On 16 April he became the hottest property in world cricket as he plundered England's attack for 375 runs, breaking Garry Sobers's long-standing record for the highest score in Test-match history.

Brian Lara's start to the 1994 season in England was, however, very nearly delayed. At the end of the Test series against England he was due to fly to London from the Caribbean, accompanied by MJK Smith, who had taken Brian's passport in order to sort out all the necessary travel documents. On the morning of departure, however, as MJK prepared to leave his room in the hotel, he couldn't find the passport anywhere. With the clock ticking down towards the final checking-in time at the airport, MJK frantically went through drawers, suitcases and wastepaper baskets for the umpteenth time – but all to no avail. Dispirited and exhausted, he finally slumped down on the second bed in the room, and, from underneath a pile of clothes he had yet to pack, out slid Brian Lara's passport. They finally made it to the airport with less than five minutes to spare.

For the next six months, along with Warwickshire supporters and every cricket fan in the country, I had the great privilege of witnessing the 'Brian Lara Phenomenon'. With his electric anticipation, quickness of eye, deftness of touch and lightning speed of movement, it seemed that he had at least three shots for every delivery bowled at him. Indeed, he was the best batsman I had ever seen, by a country mile, and those with longer memories than mine regarded him as the finest player in the world since Donald Bradman.

To see my beloved Warwickshire make cricketing history during the six months of the 1994 season was undoubtedly the highlight of my career in the game. Winning 11 of our 17 matches, we stormed to the County Championship title, finishing above runners-up Leicestershire by the record-breaking margin of 42 points.

Brian Lara's contribution to our success was immense; in the Championship he scored nine centuries, seven of them in consecutive matches. His record-breaking 501 not out against Durham, including no fewer than ten 6s and sixty-two 4s, was the perfect illustration of the way he dominated attacks throughout the summer. His arrival at the club had already tripled the size of our membership and sponsorship poured in. Crowds came thronging to Edgbaston in the hope of seeing him bat, and by the end of the season our profits from gate receipts had doubled on the previous year. It was, undoubtedly, a great time to be around the club, as everyone in the city wanted to be associated with us.

Our success in the Championship, however, was by no means a one-man affair. Among the other batsmen, Andy Moles and Roger Twose both scored double-centuries and averaged over 50 for the season in first-class cricket. There was also strong support from Trevor Penney, who had an excellent season with the bat, and Dominic Ostler – the best fielder in the club's history – whose 186 against Yorkshire at Scarborough was an innings of genuine class. In addition, Keith Piper, who kept wicket quite brilliantly throughout the summer, also came to the party with the bat, scoring his second first-class century against Durham, and sharing in a stand of over 300 runs with Brian Lara.

In the end, though, it doesn't matter how many runs a side scores; you can't win matches – let alone the Championship – if you can't bowl the opposition out. And throughout the summer that's exactly what the Warwickshire attack did. Led by Tim Munton, who enjoyed his best-ever season with 81 first-class wickets, our bowlers more than rose to the challenge. Richard Davis, the left-arm spinner newly signed from Kent, had an excellent first season, bowling us to victory with 5-wicket hauls against Yorkshire and Gloucestershire, while Gladstone Small, Paul and Neil Smith, Dermot Reeve and Graham Welch all produced match-winning spells when required.

The only fly in the ointment during our Championship-winning summer was the disappointing form of Dermot Reeve. He had begun the 1994 season as captain in all competitions. By the end of June, however, he was averaging just 12 with the bat and had taken only 7 wickets in County Championship matches. With Graham Welch consistently scoring runs and taking wickets in the 2nd XI, we were faced with a real dilemma. In the end it fell to me to tell poor Dermot that we were dropping him from the four-day side, and that Tim Munton was taking over the captaincy on a temporary basis in his absence.

In spite of his loss of form in the longer form of the game, Dermot batted and bowled as well as ever in one-day competitions. He was, for example, man of the match in the semi-final of the Benson & Hedges Cup against Surrey, taking three critical wickets for not many runs and seeing us home to victory with a typically unconventional 46 not out.

Many lesser men might have allowed the disappointment of being dropped from the Championship side to sour their relationship with the club. To his great credit, however, Dermot's upbeat enthusiasm, on and off the field, was undiminished. Moreover, his leadership in all three one-day competitions was inspirational and astute; his decision to field first whenever he won the toss, for example, undoubtedly played to the side's strength as a batting unit that could chase any target against any attack. It was a tactic that had helped us win the 1993 NatWest Trophy and it proved successful once again at Lord's on 9 July when we beat Worcestershire by a conclusive 6-wicket margin in the Benson & Hedges Cup Final.

As we entered the final fortnight of the season, everyone at the club was aware we could be about to make cricketing history. We already had the Benson & Hedges Cup on display in the trophy cabinet at Edgbaston, but we were also in an almost unassailable position at the top of the County Championship; we had a narrow lead in the AXA Equity and Law League and we were in the final of the NatWest Trophy for the second year running. No one had ever done the 'treble' before, and here we were facing the very real possibility of winning a 'quadruple'.

Rarely had I felt so helpless: as a player I had been actively involved in the unfolding drama of a match or a series and had enjoyed a degree of control over events; as an administrator I had none. My contribution had been to the building of the team and its supporting staff in the years and months leading up to this moment, and there was now nothing more I could do than hope that the players shared my burning ambition for success.

The last match of the 1994 season was in Bristol against Gloucestershire in the AXA Equity and Law League; a win guaranteed us the Sunday title and a historic treble. Alas, by this time our race to four titles was over: we had lost the NatWest final at Lord's on 4 September in a match reversing our fortunes in the Benson & Hedges final earlier in July. On a muggy September morning, Worcestershire used our own tactics against us and, having won the toss, elected to bowl on a green, seamers' paradise.

It was, however, a different story on the final Sunday of the season at Bristol, and although Gloucestershire followed Worcestershire's example by putting us in to bat, everyone was up for the challenge and none more so than Dermot Reeve. He ended the season in swaggering style with a run-a-minute 50 that swung the entire momentum of the match our way. Great credit was also due to Trevor Penney, who made a more circumspect half-century, having come to the wicket with our score at a perilous 3–3.

There was a good crowd of loyal Warwickshire supporters at Bristol to witness Dermot Reeve lifting the AXA Equity and Law League trophy. Many of them had followed us all summer and I was delighted that – after so many lean years – they were there to celebrate winning the treble with us. I was also quietly pleased that our final victory had been made possible by excellent contributions from some of our unsung heroes. In support of Dermot Reeve and Trevor Penney's batting, Tim Munton, Paul and Neil Smith, Gladstone Small, Richard Davis and Graham Welch had all held their nerve under intense pressure, bowling with Scrooge-like meanness to give us the victory and our third title of the season.

My dad Vic Amiss, back row, fourth from the right.

LAURIE COOPER. QUAINTON } FISCALI : CO : UK

BACK ROW
ALF USHER   FRANK ?   ?   VIC AMISS   FRANK COOK   HOWARD JONES
. CARVER

FRONT ROW
DEA   ?   LES MURRALL   FREDDIE   CLIFF   LAURIE COOPER.
     BRIAN PEEKS

RALPH JONES (SON OF HOWARD BACK ROW)
GEORGE

Our wedding day.

Opening partners: Geoffrey Boycott and I.

Me with the 1972 MCC England touring party to India.

Me on my way to 186 vs Pakistan at the Oval, 1974.

Me nicking one for 4 off Dennis Lillee on my way to 90 at Melbourne in 1975.

The chief executive: me in my office at Edgbaston.

Celebrating my 100th century, 1986. (Getty Images)

Getting the MBE: me with my medal, 1987.

Bringing the treble home: Jill and me with the 1994 trophies.

A pair of Brummie boys: Jasper
Carrott and I enjoy a joke.

Me with other members of 'The 100
Hundreds Club'.

Old adversaries becoming friends: Dennis Lillee and me.

The Ashes are forgotten: enjoying a drink with England's John Snow and Derek Underwood, Australia's Max Walker.

Friends Reunited: Jill and I catch up with Tony and Vivian Greig

A pioneer of women's cricket: me with Rachael Heyhoe Flint.

Jill and I celebrating our fiftieth wedding anniversary with the family.

Celebrating my Honorary
Doctorate, 2007.

Jill and I with Giles Clarke at a presentation upon my
retirement from the ECB, 2011.

15

Doing the 'Double', Drugs and Development

Early on in the 1994 season I discovered that a bookmaker called Surrey Racing was offering bets on county cricket teams winning multiple trophies. The odds being given against Warwickshire winning two trophies and getting to the final of the other two competitions were so long that I thought it might be a bit of fun to have a flutter.

In those days there were no regulations preventing players or administrators from placing bets on matches or series involving their own sides, and I wondered if MJK Smith might be interested in joining me for a speculative wager.

'I'm up for that,' he said, when I'd explained the details. 'I'll put £50 on it if you will.'

'What about the rest of the committee?' I asked.

'You'd better ask them,' he replied. 'Bring it up at the next meeting.'

By the end of the week ten of us had formed a syndicate and placed a bet with Surrey Racing that we estimated would win us a grand total of £250,000.

The prospect of the team reaching the goal required by the bookmakers for a payout seemed so remote, however, that none of us gave the bet a second thought until the end of August. At that point, with the Benson & Hedges already in the bag, the team at the top of the Championship and AXA tables, and a place in the final of the NatWest competition, everyone in the syndicate began to wonder if 'mission impossible' might actually be fulfilled.

The day after our victory over Gloucestershire in the final AXA Equity and Law League match of the season, I rang Surrey Racing to make arrangements for the payment of our winnings.

'I'm sorry, Mr Amiss,' said the voice on the end of the line. 'I think there must be a misunderstanding. Your syndicate has won nowhere near £250,000. If you read the small print on the betting form you will see that it was a "speciality bet" with a maximum payout of £50,000.'

Our main disappointment was that we had always intended to give the team an equal share of the spoils; it was, after all, their success on the field that had made our unlikely win possible. Nonetheless, we were able to give the squad an unexpected, but well deserved, £5,000 bonus to share out between them.

Meanwhile, with the season over, we bade a sad farewell to Brian Lara; his impact on the club in the six months of the summer had been astonishing. He had finished top of the national first-class batting averages by a huge distance, with 2,066 runs in 15 matches at an average of 89.82. Of even greater significance, however, was the fact that he had scored his runs at a rate that not only demoralised opposition bowlers, but also gave us ample time to bowl sides out.

The only downside to his time at Edgbaston was that, other than on match days, he was rarely around. His record-breaking innings of 375 during the Antigua Test match in March had made him hot property commercially, and both Brian and his agent were anxious to take financial advantage of his celebrity status. As a result, he spent most of his spare time during the summer being driven from one promotional event to another. Although this often meant missing practice sessions, we didn't feel in a position to object – we had, after all, signed him for a fee that was well below his commercial value.

Halfway through the season one of the more senior players came to talk to me about the impact that Brian's other commitments were having on his appearances at practice sessions that everyone else was expected to attend. 'We know that all his promotional work isn't affecting his performance on the field,' he said. 'That's not the point. The fact is, though, that he's rarely ever around and, when he is, he's too busy with his agent arranging his next sponsorship deal to spend any time with us. Don't get me wrong, Dennis,' he added, 'Brian's a lovely guy and a great player, but we don't want him to become isolated from the rest of the team.'

Having listened to the players' point of view, I was concerned that, unless something was done, a rift might develop between Brian and the rest of the team. With this in mind, I was anxious to meet with him as soon as possible to discuss and, hopefully, resolve the situation.

When I eventually got through to him on the phone he suggested that we meet at the Belfry Golf Club at 9 a.m. the following day. I duly arrived on time to discover that he had just started a lesson with the club's pro. I waited in the clubhouse, and an hour later he strolled off the practice green, oblivious of the time.

'Do you fancy a round of golf, Dennis?' he asked, flashing the smile that always brought instant forgiveness for any transgression.

'I'm not sure that will be possible,' I replied. 'Members have to book a teeing-off time. I don't think we can just barge in.'

'Don't worry about that,' said the pro, who had come off the practice green with him. 'You can tee off when you like; anyone who's booked that time slot will just have to wait.'

Such was the aura that surrounded Brian Lara; just as he had torn up all the conventional rules of batting with his gloriously innovative strokeplay, so, off the field, it seemed that the regulations that the rest of us had to observe did not apply to him. It wasn't that he was in any way arrogant or self-regarding; it was just that, as far as he was concerned, there were no limitations on what he might achieve, and his winning charm was utterly irresistible.

It wasn't until the ninth hole of our round that I broached the subject that I had come to discuss. Brian was already four holes up and playing like the champion he might well have been had he chosen golf over cricket. Indeed, as the season progressed I came to realise that he was good at pretty much everything he did.

I was aware as I opened the conversation that I had to tread very carefully indeed; while I had a duty of care to the other players, and an obligation to articulate their feelings and fears, I also needed to voice their concerns in a way that didn't alienate Brian within the dressing room. My aim was to unite rather than divide, and so I did my best to avoid any suggestion of blame or criticism.

Whatever I said worked, in the sense that Brian was not in the slightest bit offended and, to his credit, agreed to make an effort to spend more time with the rest of the team. What's more, for a few weeks he definitely tried to be 'one of the boys' but, in the final analysis, it wasn't in his DNA. What made him such a remarkable batsman was the same distinctive individuality that was evident in the way he lived his life away from the game: you could not have one without the other.

Most cricketing pundits believed that there was no way we could match the astonishing achievements of the 1994 'treble' season without Brian Lara, and they were proved right: in 1995 we only managed the 'double' – winning the County Championship and the NatWest Trophy. Although we finished joint top of the AXA Equity and Law League with Kent, we were denied the title, and a second consecutive 'treble', because of Kent's marginally better run rate per 100 balls over the season.

It was nonetheless a remarkable effort and not only were we runaway winners in the Championship for the second year running, but we actually improved on our performance of the previous year by winning 14 – as compared to 13 – of our 17 matches.

The most satisfying aspect of our achievement in 1995 was that it finally dispelled the myth that our success had been based on the performances of one player. Indeed, the key to retaining the Championship title and winning the NatWest for the second time in three seasons was the strength in depth of our playing squad.

One of the things that pleased me most was the return to both form and captaincy of Dermot Reeve in the four-day game. Following his disappointing season with bat and ball in 1994, he bounced back with Tigger-like verve in the County Championship, averaging just under 40 with the bat, and taking a hatful of wickets at less than 18 runs a piece. Moreover, in the NatWest final against Northamptonshire he won the man of the match award for his all-round performance and leadership. Putting himself on to bowl at the most pressurised time towards the end of the Northamptonshire innings, Dermot took the critical wicket of David Capel and dried up the opposition run rate. He then saw us home to victory with an undefeated 37.

Although Brian Lara was not with us for the 1995 season, I began to realise, as the summer progressed, that he had left an invaluable legacy with us: he seemed to have passed on his insatiable thirst for big scores to our other batsmen. Roger Twose and Trevor Penney both scored four centuries in County Championship matches, and Dominic Ostler topped an impressive hundred against Essex with a magnificent double-century at Edgbaston against a strong Surrey attack. We also saw the continued development of Nick Knight as a player of real quality and ambition, and his consistency in the Championship throughout 1995 earned him selection for England against the West Indies.

With the batsmen all in form, the shortage of runs that some had predicted did not materialise. What's more, our bowling attack was undoubtedly strengthened by the return of Allan Donald as our overseas player. Unlike some fast bowlers who cruise when the conditions are not ideal for them, Allan gave his all every time he bowled. He took 5-wicket hauls on no fewer than six occasions, and there were times when he was almost unplayable.

Allan was magnificently supported throughout the summer by Tim Munton, Gladstone Small, Paul Smith and Dermot Reeve, and with Graham Welch and Dougie Brown also in the squad, we had, unquestionably, the strongest seam attack in the country. As a result, opposition sides were regularly dismissed for less than 150; Glamorgan were bowled out twice in the match for 122, we blew Yorkshire away on a flat wicket at Edgbaston for 96, and skittled out Leicestershire at Grace Road for a mere 67.

What pleased me most during the season, however, was the support the players gave to each other. This was evident in the camaraderie of the dressing room, and in the athleticism and focus of the fielding during matches. Keith Piper was in superb form behind the stumps, and the slip catching of Nick Knight and Dominic Ostler was of the highest standard. Thus, the bowlers could deliver the ball, confident that if the batsman got an outside edge he'd be on his way back to the pavilion. At the end of the season not only had Keith Piper got more dismissals than any other wicketkeeper in the country, but Nick Knight, with 29 catches, and Dominic Ostler, with 25, were also the leading fielders in the Championship.

In all, the 1st XI won eight titles in all competitions between 1993 and 2002 – The NatWest Trophy in 1993 and 1995, the County Championship in 1994 and 1995, the Benson & Hedges Cup in 1994 and 2002, and the variously named Sunday League competitions in 1994, 1997 – and people often ask me which of these achievements was the most satisfying. It is a question that I simply cannot answer because each of them was achieved under different circumstances, and in some cases with different personnel.

Having said that, there was a ninth title that was of special significance to me. In 1996 we won the 2nd XI County Championship with a young team that included Mark Wagh, Michael Powell, Tony Frost and Ashley Giles. While drinking champagne with the 1st XI after their various title victories was a great joy, watching this new generation of players develop and grow to maturity was a more lasting pleasure.

The man responsible for overseeing the development of the 2nd XI during my time as chief executive was Neal Abberley. He knew the game inside out, having had played over 250 first-class games for Warwickshire, and been a fellow member of the under-25 MCC touring team to Pakistan in 1966/67. Quiet and undemonstrative, he was, above all, an astute judge of players; it was Neal, for example, who persuaded us to sign Ashley Giles after he had been rejected by Surrey. He was also the man to whom Ian Bell has attributed much of his considerable success as a Test player. His respect was such that, when Neal tragically died in 2011, Ian persuaded the England team to join him in wearing black armbands in his honour during the Test against India at Edgbaston in the days following his death.

As time went by, there were inevitable comings and goings in personnel; Bob Woolmer left us as coach after the 1995 'double' season to become the coach of South Africa. He returned to Edgbaston for two seasons from 2000 to 2002 and was followed by John Inverarity, a deeply thoughtful former headmaster who had also played Test cricket for Australia. Although more conventional in his approach than Bob, he was a superb coach who encouraged the players to think deeply about the game.

John was a calming influence in a crisis and could always be relied on to keep things simple. He also liked to deliver clear and unambiguous messages to the players. During one tea interval at Edgbaston, after a poor session, the bowlers were told to assemble and did so, expecting some subtle strategic advice on what they needed to do to get back in the game.

'Guys, let's try something different after tea,' he said. 'Three points. Bowl a line and length. Bowl a line and length. Bowl a f★★★★★★ line and length.' The message was clear.

In 2004, John's second season as coach, we won the Championship for the sixth time in the club's history. Led brilliantly by Nick Knight, who had taken over the captaincy from Mike Powell, we went through the summer unbeaten. It was a great season during which our Australian overseas player, Brad Hogg, played a central role. He was a hugely positive influence in the dressing room and scored a lot of runs very quickly. Ian Bell also made a significant contribution to our victory, scoring six centuries and forcing his way into the England Test side.

I cannot claim, however, that everything that happened in my time in charge at Edgbaston went as planned. The return of Brian Lara as captain in 1998, for example, was nowhere near as successful as we hoped it would be. He was still the hottest property in world cricket and, as a consequence, throughout the summer he had an impossible schedule of promotion events to combine with his responsibilities as a player and captain. On one occasion, for example, Phil Neale – the coach at the time – rang me from Harrogate to say that Brian had still not arrived with half an hour to go before he was due to toss up with the opposition skipper. I quickly rang the house we rented for Brian in the city, and much to my surprise he replied.

'Brian,' I said. 'You're supposed to be in Harrogate.'

'I've had a bit of business to see to,' he said. 'I'm just about to leave. I won't be long.'

'Do you know how far Harrogate is?' I replied. 'It's the best part of 150 miles away.'

To be fair to Brian, he was as disappointed as we were that we couldn't reproduce the magic of 1994, and although he went back to the Caribbean on this occasion without the euphoria of success, he still has a very special place in Warwickshire's history.

For the most part, however, we managed to appoint the right people to key positions. The major challenge was to motivate everyone in the club, irrespective of whether they worked in the office or were Test stars like Brian Lara or Allan Donald. I had seen, when playing under the captaincy of Mike Brearley, how it was possible to get the very best out of people by treating them as valued individuals rather than members of a regiment who needed to be drilled to ensure uniformity. The most important thing, it seemed to me, was to treat everyone at the club with care and consideration.

Having begun my career in a hierarchical era when junior players were seen but not heard, I felt strongly that I had to give as much time and thought to those struggling on the fringes as I gave to the stars of the side. Indeed, the only thing that kept me awake at night during my time as chief executive was knowing that, in the morning, I would have to inform a member of the playing staff that he was being released at the end of the season.

Although the decision to release a player was made by the cricket committee, it was my job to communicate this to the individuals concerned. I knew from my own personal experience that the final few weeks of the summer are an anxious time, particularly for those who are short of runs or wickets. The apprehension that some feel prior to hearing their fate is such that they simply don't process what is being said. This was clearly evident on one occasion when a particularly nervous young player – who shall remain nameless – came to my office for his end of season meeting.

'Good morning, X,' I said, trying as hard as I could to hide my own nervousness. 'Thank you for coming to see me. I want to talk to you about your future.'

I could already see from the glazed look in his eyes that X was with me in body only; his mind was clearly elsewhere. Nonetheless, he had to be told what had been decided by the cricket committee, and so I continued.

'You've been with us three seasons now and we've decided – rightly or wrongly – that it wouldn't be in your best interests to offer you another contract for next season.'

'That's great,' he replied. 'Thank you.'

'Did you hear me properly?' I asked, dumbfounded by his ecstatic reaction. 'We're not renewing your contract; we're letting you go. You won't be on the playing staff here at Edgbaston next season.'

There was a brief pause as the reality of his situation dawned on him, and then he broke down in floods of tears.

While X was emotionally devastated by the news, there were others who responded with anger and a sense of injustice. No matter how they reacted, however, my role was to help them move on to the next phase of their lives, either by contacting other clubs on their behalf so they could continue their playing careers elsewhere, or by introducing them to potential employers outside the game.

Our commitment to supporting players at times of personal crisis was central to the way in which we dealt with Keith Piper's failure to pass a drugs test in 2005. Bob Woolmer had made me aware during his second term as coach at Warwickshire, between 2000 and 2002, that there was talk in the dressing room about the use of recreational drugs. As a result we initiated a package of measures, including educational workshops and the introduction of our own drugs tests.

In spite of this – and within a year of each other – two of our players, Graham Wagg and Keith Piper, were both found to have used illegal substances. In Graham Wagg's case, the fact that he had taken cocaine, a Class A drug, meant that the ECB gave him an automatic two-season ban. This left Warwickshire with no alternative but to terminate his contract as a player. To his credit, though, Graham (who was only 21 at the time) has rebuilt his career and his reputation with Derbyshire and more recently with Glamorgan.

Keith Piper, however, was 35 when he failed a routine drugs test in 2005. The laboratory analysis revealed that he had taken cannabis, a Class C drug. Unsurprisingly, the ECB banned him from playing for four months, and we made the decision to release him on the basis that it was his second offence; he had, in fact, been banned previously in 1997 after failing an in-house test.

I have never quite understood why shockwaves ran through the game when it was discovered that some professional cricketers were experimenting with illegal substances. The research undertaken by Mentor UK some years ago, for example, revealed that by the age of 15, 37 per cent of teenagers have taken cannabis. The question that this raises is why cricketers should be an exception. Indeed, if young players are as likely to have experimented with the drug as any other people of the same age, then it is only surprising that more cricketers have not tested positive.

The fact that several ex-players, including our own Paul Smith and Dermot Reeve, have subsequently confessed to the use of recreational drugs during their cricketing careers also suggests that the problem is more widespread than many would like to admit.

As far as I was concerned, there were two central issues that needed to be addressed in the event of a player failing a drugs test. On the one hand, we had to support the ECB's recreational drug policy in an attempt to keep the game 'clean'; on the other, we had a duty of care towards our players and a clear responsibility to support them in times of crisis.

Keith Piper's situation was particularly difficult. It was inevitable that sanctions would be taken against him in order to deter other players from following his example. Had he been in his early 20s, the termination of his contract would not have been quite so serious; he was such a brilliant wicketkeeper that counties would have been queuing up to sign him once he had completed his ban. At 35 years of age, however, this was highly unlikely, and I was concerned that without proper help Keith's life could unravel and fall apart.

It was because of these fears that we joined forces with the ECB and the Professional Cricketers' Association in putting together a rehabilitation programme, including counselling, career advice and financial support.

There were, of course, those who criticised our approach as being too liberal and permissive. They argued that there should be 'zero tolerance' of drugs, and that those caught should be banned for life from any involvement in the game – playing, coaching or administration.

My view has always been that there is no place for drugs either in cricket or in wider society. I also agree that sanctions are necessary as a deterrent. Nevertheless, in my experience, the players who have transgressed by using illegal substances have been among the most vulnerable and, therefore, the most in need of a helping hand. In all conscience, I don't believe it would be right to wash our hands of them.

By the time the drug scandal broke at Warwickshire in 2005, I had been with the club either as a player, committee member or administrator for a total of thirty-seven years. Many things had changed in that time: the growing popularity of shorter versions of the game, including T20; developments in clothing and equipment; the influence of satellite television; levels of prize money and financial remuneration; the introduction of floodlights and night cricket. There was now even talk about new technology being introduced to provide a decision review system for umpires.

In my view, the vast majority of these developments were positive and indicative of cricket's increasing responsiveness to a changing world. Yes: the drug issues that we encountered at Edgbaston in 2005 were damaging for the image of the game and the individuals concerned, but in spite of it, during the same summer, cricket fans were treated to one of the finest Test series ever played, as Michael Vaughan's unfancied England side won the Ashes with some scintillating displays of team and individual brilliance.

The game was back where it belonged in the public imagination, and the fears that innovations such as the introduction of T20 cricket would destroy the fundamental traditions of cricket were proving groundless.

As early as 1997 we had been in the vanguard of a new era in one-day cricket at Edgbaston, hosting the first senior limited-overs match to be played under floodlights. The occasion attracted a crowd of over 18,000, including large numbers of families, who all enjoyed a wonderful evening's entertainment as Warwickshire beat Somerset by 35 runs.

Nine years on from that pioneering event, as the 2006 season drew to a close, I retired as chief executive at Edgbaston after more than a decade in charge. It had been an immensely fulfilling experience, during which the team had enjoyed unprecedented success on the field. There had also been significant developments of the ground and stadium, with the rebuilding of the Eric Hollies Stand and the completion of the RES Wyatt Stand, housing additional seating, executive boxes and two pitch-side restaurants.

Aside from the day-to-day contact with all the people at the club, one of the things I had always loved most about Edgbaston was the crowd's wonderful sense of humour – exemplified, in particular, by the sparkling wit that always seemed to come out of the Hollies Stand. One of my favourite moments took place in an ODI during the World Cup. Aaron Finch, the Australian all-rounder, was fielding on the boundary in front of the stand and was getting the stick especially reserved for Aussie opponents every time he walked back towards the crowd. It eventually got to him and, in an attempt to avoid any more comments, he made his way towards the boundary ropes with his back to the stand. In an instant the whole Hollies contingent joined in an impersonation of a vehicle reversing: 'Beep, beep, beep, beep, beep, beep,' they all yelled – leaving the rest of the Edgbaston crowd crying with laughter.

It was because of moments like this that I knew – even though the time had come for me to relinquish the reins of the club – that Edgbaston would continue to be my 'home from home' for the rest of my life. Meanwhile, though, at the end of 2006 it was time for me to move on. I had been a member of the board at the ECB since 2001 and now I had an opportunity to help shape the future direction of the game at a national and international level.

16

Pioneering Policy, Pitfalls and Pietersen

On taking up my appointment as CEO of Warwickshire in 1994, I had automatically become a member of the ECB's forerunner, the TCCB. Comprising the various chairmen and chief executives of all eighteen first-class counties, together with representatives from the Minor Counties and various other cricketing organisations, it was a large and unwieldy committee. With the interests of the smaller counties often in tension with the bigger clubs, there was rarely a consensus and, as a result, important decisions were often deferred or simply shelved. It was also never entirely clear what the parameters of the TCCB's authority actually were. Along with the Cricket Council and the National Cricket Association, it was one of three organisations responsible for the governance of the game.

As we moved towards a new millennium, there was a growing recognition that the way cricket was run was more akin to the feudal system of the Middle Ages than to the needs of the modern era. The England Test side was struggling to compete with Australia, the West Indies, India and the emerging South African side. Crowds for County Championship matches were disappearing fast and the game was dwindling in schools.

The extent to which cricket was out of step with the modern world was exemplified by MCC's refusal to admit women as members of the club until 1998: fully twenty-three years after the first Sex Discrimination Act had become law in the UK. As far as I was concerned reform was long overdue, and I was proud to second Brian Johnstone's proposal of Rachael Heyhoe Flint as one of the first ten women to become members of MCC in 1999.

In spite of some reactionary opposition, the reorganisation of the jurisdiction and administration of cricket's establishment began in 1997 with the founding of the ECB as the single controlling body of the game throughout England, Northern Ireland and Wales. With a slimmed-down governing body, it was designed to be more decisive, proactive and flexible; within just twelve months the newly formed ECB was demonstrating a far more enlightened outlook, and one of its first and most important steps was to take responsibility for developing cricket as a sport for women.

As a former player, I had been appointed to the board to advise on cricketing matters (as opposed to areas such as finance or marketing) and, before becoming vice-chair in 2007, I spent three years as chair of cricket and a similar period as chair of the England management committee.

The first real challenge that I faced as chair of cricket was helping the board decide how to replace the Benson & Hedges Cup that was due to end in 2002. There was no doubt in my mind that we needed another one-day competition to fill its place in the cricketing calendar. I was of the view, however, that it was time to experiment with something new and different. While crowds had been drawn in the early days of the Gillette Cup, support for one-day competitions, including the Sunday League, had fallen away considerably by the turn of the millennium. Because of this, I felt that we needed something revolutionary to bring energy and excitement back into cricket grounds.

The solution came as a result of market research conducted on behalf of the ECB. The aim of the survey was to provide the board with objective evidence about families and their recreational interests, including critical questions about the ideal time of day and duration of the activities that they were most likely to support and become involved in.

The two key findings were that, for the vast majority of people, the optimum time to engage in recreational pursuits was after work or school, and the maximum duration was three hours. In addition, however, the survey confirmed that there was a shortage of opportunities across the country for parents and their children to share in experiences and events at times that suited the pattern of family life. It was in this context that we created a new version of the game that was unashamedly designed to make cricket accessible to families and, in particular, to a younger generation who had been switched off by four- and five-day cricket.

After much hard debate, planning and controversy, the first matches in a new 20-over competition, the T20 Cup, took place on 13 June 2003. Much to the horror of the traditionalists, the promotion of the competition followed the marketing strategy that was so successful for Kerry Packer twenty-five years previously. Using the slogan 'I don't like cricket, I love it' – a line from the cricket-themed pop song 'Dreadlock Holiday' by 10cc – the cricketing establishment finally embraced the branding and advertising techniques of contemporary commerce and industry.

While the first season of T20 in England was a success, with a full house watching the Surrey Lions defeat the Warwickshire Bears in the final at Trent Bridge by 9 wickets, the second year's competition was an absolute triumph. In the first ever T20 match played at Lord's on 15 July 2004, a crowd of 26,500 thronged to see Middlesex play Surrey in a group match. It was the biggest crowd that had attended a county cricket fixture, other than a one-day final, since 1953.

As far as I was concerned, T20 was the shot in the arm that cricket in England had needed for two decades, and I was proud to have been involved at the ECB in its inception and development. There were, of course, many critics who believed that it would undermine the fabric of the traditional game. I would argue, however, that for the majority of cricketers who began playing the game in limited-over matches after school, T20 represents a return to cricket's traditional roots and not a departure from it. My only sadness is that having invented such a dynamic and popular shorter version of our sport, the ECB lost control of it to the Indian cricket authorities.

The success of T20 in England had been the envy of every cricketing country, and it shouldn't have come as any great surprise to us at the ECB when Lalit Modi – vice-president of the Indian Cricket Board – approached us to discuss plans for a Champions League T20 tournament to begin in India in 2008. The competition was to feature the top domestic teams from the leading Test-playing nations, and he invited the ECB to work in partnership with India, Australia and South Africa as joint owners of the Champions League, in return for a 25 per cent share of the profits.

The decision not to join forces with Lalit Modi's cricketing consortium was unfortunate. Not only did it leave the ECB isolated and without influence in a version of the game it had created, but it also meant the loss of revenue from a commercially successful venture.

In many ways, the introduction of the new 100-ball game in England in 2020 is the consequence of having lost control of the T20 format of cricket. Whether it is sufficiently different from T20 to generate the new crowds it needs remains to be seen, but it will at least enable the ECB to have exclusive rights over its own game.

Although much time was given to researching, planning and implementing the T20 competition in my early years on the board, the drive to make England a successful Test side was always a major priority. And while winning the 2005 Ashes series was a highlight for everyone involved, there was no escaping the implications of the disastrous 5–0 whitewash in the 2006/07 series in Australia. It was the first time England had suffered such a humiliating drubbing since the 1920/21 Ashes series. The dismal performances on the field, and the stories of hard drinking and late-night parties off it, led the board to the inevitable conclusion that things had to change.

Realising we needed the objective perspective of someone unconnected with cricket, we commissioned Ken Schofield – the former director of the European PGA Tour – to be the fresh pair of eyes through which we might see things more clearly. The 200-page report that he produced made nineteen specific recommendations that became the basis for the most radical changes in the history of the game in England and Wales.

As far as the development of international cricket in England was concerned, the most significant changes were the introduction of central contracts for recognised Test players and the creation of an England performance squad for those on the fringes of international cricket.

Both measures had my full support, and I was confident they would provide players with a sense of security and belonging that was so clearly missing when I first played for England. I was also quite certain that the fast bowlers, in particular, would benefit enormously from a system designed to protect them from being over-bowled in an endless succession of County Championship matches. Indeed, the longevity of James Anderson and Stuart Broad's careers in the top flight of the game is clear evidence that central contracts have been a great success.

The Schofield Report also heralded a revolution in the individually tailored training, skill set preparation and medical support given to players from Academy status to Test level. In this context, the refurbishment and rebranding of the National Cricket Centre at Loughborough, the emphasis on international exchanges for emerging players, and the wholesale reorganisation and allocation of coaching resources, were fundamental in our drive to raise standards throughout the game.

In essence, Ken Schofield concluded that, if England were to stand a chance of becoming the no. 1 cricketing nation in the world, we had to abandon the outmoded, amateur attitudes that had continued to dominate the game since the nineteenth century. And central to his whole plan was a radical restructuring of the way in which the Test and ODI sides were chosen and managed.

What he recognised was that the old cricket committee system that had relied on the part-time goodwill of former players and administrators was no longer fit for purpose. His recommendation was to appoint a full-time, professional, cricketing management team responsible to the ECB for the selection and performance of the England cricket team.

From a personal point of view, the Schofield Report was a great relief. As chairman of the ECB's cricket committee at the time, I was not only responsible for policy matters relating to the England cricket team, but I was also doing much of the day-to-day work that is now undertaken on a full-time basis by the managing director of England's men's cricket. It was a classic case of governance and executive roles becoming confused.

The appointment in 2007 of the successful businessman Giles Clarke as chairman of the ECB intensified the drive for change, and all of the nineteen recommendations included in Ken Schofield's report were accepted without quibble or amendment.

Although my role as chair of cricket became subsumed by the new managing director's post, I soon found myself busier than ever when I was elected as Giles Clarke's vice-chairman. His role was to oversee the business and commercial interests of the board, while I continued to have prime responsibility for cricketing issues.

My first and most important role as vice-chairman was to help and advise in the appointment of Hugh Morris in 2007 as managing director of England cricket, and then of Andy Flower as coach of England's Test and ODI sides. I was also closely involved in the decision in 2008 to invite Geoff Miller to take over as chairman of the England selection committee from David Graveney, who had fulfilled the role for over ten years, often in very difficult circumstances.

My experience as CEO at Edgbaston had taught me that the key to achieving success in any organisation is getting the right people in place. In Geoff Miller, Hugh Morris and Andy Flower we had the perfect team to rebuild England's fortunes following the disastrous 5–0 Ashes defeat in 2006/07.

Geoff Miller proved to be a brilliant chairman of selectors; widely respected for his deep knowledge and experience of the game at the highest level, he brought a combination of thoughtfulness, energy and sparkling wit to the role. He was the perfect foil to Hugh Morris, who led the management team with quiet authority, diplomacy and great intelligence. He showed great judgement in developing clear parameters between his role as managing director and Andy Flower's responsibilities as coach. While he was always closely involved in decisions about how, when and where the team would be training, he never allowed interest and engagement to become interference. Indeed, there was no need to interfere – Andy was an excellent coach who was tactically and technically very astute. Although quietly spoken and undemonstrative he commanded the respect of the players, whom he treated with courtesy and consideration. Above all, though, he established a culture in which players took personal responsibility for their own performances.

The changes in the ECB's management structure and personnel began to bear fruit in 2009 during the Test series against Ricky Ponting's Australian touring side. Under Andrew Strauss's captaincy, the side played with the kind of steel and ambition that had been missing since the historic Ashes victory of 2005. There was also a sense of purpose and direction in the way England played that reflected the meticulous and detailed planning that Andy Flower had already put in place.

A nail-biting win in the final Test at the Oval gave us a 2–1 series victory and a great sense of satisfaction that all the training and preparation had been rewarded. While I was delighted for the players, the coaching team and the selectors, I was also very proud of the planning and hard work the board had done behind the scenes at the ECB in laying the foundations for success.

The sole objective in introducing radical reforms at the ECB had been to raise standards on the field of play, and confirmation that this was being achieved came with a 3–1 series victory in the 2010/11 Ashes series. To win at home in England was one thing, but defeating an Australian side in their own country was something that had not been achieved for over twenty years.

It was prior to this tour that the board and management team involved the players' wives, partners and girlfriends in discussions about how to minimise the impact of the tour on relationships and family life. It was a far cry from the attitude taken by the powers-that-be during the 1974/75 Ashes tour, and I was delighted that Andrew Strauss's squad and their loved ones would not be subjected to the twenty-one-day rule that had caused such ill feeling in the past.

It was not, however, all plain sailing during my time on the board at the ECB, and there is no doubt that we made some mistakes. The most public and embarrassing of these became known as the 'Stanford Scandal'.

A Texan billionaire, Allen Stanford, was the most unlikely of cricket fans; he first came to the ECB's attention in 2006 when he pumped $38 million into a Caribbean T20 tournament in his name. His declared aim was to boost the game's flagging profile and reputation in the West Indies. After a second tournament in 2008, attracting a global television audience of 300 million viewers, he approached the ECB with a proposal to stage five T20 internationals between England and the West Indies, with a total prize fund of $20 million to be awarded to the team that won the championship.

It wasn't long after we had signed a highly lucrative deal that alarm bells began to ring. His ostentatious arrival in a helicopter at Lord's seemed to indicate that Allen Stanford was more interested in promoting himself than the game of cricket. Nagging doubts became firmer suspicions a few months later in the Caribbean when his behaviour with some of the England players' wives was most inappropriate.

What we didn't know, of course, was that the financial authorities in America were investigating him for fraud, and so when he was arrested shortly after the 2008 T20 series the press had a field day. There were even calls from the press for ECB chairman Giles Clarke and chief executive David Collier to resign.

With the benefit of hindsight, everyone at the ECB regretted getting involved with Allen Stanford, but the accusations that Giles Clarke and David Collier had failed to apply due diligence in researching his financial security were unfair and unfounded. For well over a decade Stanford had managed to hide his shady dealings from tax and revenue services in both America and the Caribbean. The annual accounts of his companies had always been approved by reputable auditors and, what's more, the prize money that he promised for his first tournament in 2006 was duly paid without delay. Nevertheless, we had been well and truly duped, and reminded of the old adage that 'if it sounds too good to be true, it probably is'.

As the member of the board with particular responsibility for cricketing matters, I wasn't involved in negotiating the deal with Allen Stanford, but there were certainly some tricky player/personnel issues to deal with that did fall within my area of interest – and they usually involved Kevin Pietersen.

Kevin was a batsman for whom I had the highest regard. From the moment he announced himself on the international stage during the dramatic 2005 Ashes series in England, I believed that there was a rare touch of genius about his batting. His ability to dominate world-class bowling attacks, combining classical technique with audacious improvisation, reminded me of other recent greats such as Garry Sobers, Viv Richards and Brian Lara.

The statistics of his early Test career also seemed to suggest that he would find a place in cricket's Hall of Fame. After twenty-five Tests, for example, he had scored the second-highest run total ever, behind only the legendary Sir Don Bradman. He was also the fastest player in terms of days to reach 4,000, 5,000 and 7,000 Test runs, and in 2007 he became only the third England batsman to top the ICC one-day international rankings. He was described in the *Guardian* as 'England's greatest modern batsman', and on the occasion of England's 1,000th Test in 2018 he was named in the ECB's 'Greatest England XI'.

Had Kevin been a tennis player, or indeed a golfer, he might have avoided much of the controversy that surrounded his playing career. As an individual performer on the field of play he was exceptional, but as a member of a team, in and around the dressing room, he was less successful.

Before he was selected for England there had been whispers from county dressing rooms, including his former club at Trent Bridge, that he could be arrogant, opinionated and dismissive of players with less talent than himself. In my view, however, his qualities as a world-class cricketer far outweighed the demerits of an – allegedly – oversized ego. During my Test career I had played alongside a number of characters who were never afraid to tell you how good they were. More often than not, however, firm management and clear leadership had been enough to ensure their influence wasn't divisive.

When Kevin first joined the England side Michael Vaughan was well established as the England skipper. He and the coach, Duncan Fletcher, ran a tight, disciplined ship which also allowed players to express themselves individually on the field. While they were expected to contribute to team discussions and planning off the pitch, there was never any doubt that Michael and Duncan were in overall charge of operations. This suited Kevin well – he was free to play his own game, and while it was acknowledged that he was the best batsman in the team, he was not afforded rights or status above anyone else in the side.

The problems really began to surface in 2008 when Michael Vaughan retired from Test cricket and, after eight successful years as coach, Duncan Fletcher moved on to pastures new. Kevin was by no means everyone's choice to replace Michael as captain, but he was an experienced Test player and by far the strongest personality in the side. Largely because of this, there was a feeling that he would be better leading than following. Thus it was that Kevin was made England skipper in 2008 for the Fourth Test against South Africa. Within six months, however, he was replaced by Andrew Strauss.

The catalyst for Kevin's sudden and hasty resignation as England captain was a dispute with the newly appointed coach, Peter Moores, that began during the winter tour to India. Peter had been appointed England coach after a very successful few years in a similar role at Sussex, during which they had won the Championship. He was well known to us at the ECB, having coached the England A team on the 2000/01 tour to the West Indies, and had subsequently been appointed as coach of the English National Cricket Academy.

The only thing that was missing from Peter's otherwise impeccable CV was experience of Test cricket, and most of the people closely involved with the England side at the time believe that this was the underlying issue. Rightly or wrongly, Kevin Pietersen believed that he knew more about preparing players for Test cricket than Peter Moores, and that, as captain, he should have the final say.

Kevin and Peter had stepped into a vacuum of power at the same time, and perhaps the conflict that resulted was inevitable. Understandably, both men wanted to stamp their authority on their area of operation from the outset, but with Kevin resigning in an acrimonious atmosphere and Peter asking for the ECB to back him, we were left in a quandary. The team was split down the middle: some agreed with Kevin and some sided with Peter.

Geoff Miller, Hugh Morris and I had lengthy discussions about the best way forward, and in the end we decided that the only answer was a clean sweep. The sad truth is that, without the full support of the dressing room, Peter's position had become as untenable as Kevin's.

With Peter Moores gone, I suspect that Kevin believed he would be asked to resume the captaincy. The fact that we opted to appoint Andrew Strauss as skipper was a real bone of contention, and it was probably this that culminated in Kevin sending critical text messages about Andrew to friends in the opposition side during the 2012 series against South Africa.

Throughout all the controversies that surrounded Kevin, I felt that my job was simply to ask the management if everything was being done to keep him in the fold, and I think that it may have had some influence in keeping channels of communication open.

In many ways, though, I'm glad that, having retired from the board, I was not involved in the final decision after the 2013/14 Ashes tour to dispense with his services. While I recognise the importance of team unity and a harmonious dressing room, I also know that Test cricket needs exciting and innovative players like Kevin Pietersen if it is going to survive as a spectator sport. His 158 at the Oval against Australia in 2005 was an innings of absolute genius in its power and audacity, and to deny the world such a glorious spectacle is a huge responsibility.

At the end of the 2011 season, however, it was time for me to step down from my role as vice-chairman of the ECB and bring an end to my official relationship with cricket as a player, an administrator and a trustee. It was a career and love affair that spanned seven decades and brought me friends, fun and much adventure. Indeed, the 15-year-old boy from Harborne who walked through the gates at Edgbaston on that cold April morning in 1958 on his first day as a professional cricketer never dreamed that cricket would take him round the world many times, nor that it would give him so much joy and, at times, more than a little despair.

17

Farewell, Family, Friends and Fun

When I was chief executive at Warwickshire – working long and often unsociable hours – I frequently found myself smiling with polite disbelief when older members of the club insisted that, since retiring, they had never been busier in their lives. At the end of a fraught day, particularly when we were hosting a Test match at Edgbaston, I would often find a group of superannuated seniors assembled in the pavilion bar sharing tales of their packed and busy schedules and wondering how they had ever found the time to go to work.

The mildly irritated scepticism that I felt at the time fell away within weeks of my own retirement. Indeed, the combined commitments that Jill and I now have are such that it is hard to see how we could fit much more into our lives. As a former Test player, for example, I am always being approached to give talks and award prizes at cricket societies, clubs or schools. There are also functions at Edgbaston and, although I no longer have an official role at the club, I am nonetheless always 'on duty' at these events, and thoroughly enjoy catching up with guests, visitors, former players and retired employees.

Having been active and focused all my working life, the prospect of a sedentary retirement had no appeal whatsoever. Not that I needed to worry; since stepping down from the board at the ECB in 2011,

I have – like the older members at Edgbaston I used to chuckle at – been as busy, if not busier, than I was before. The only difference is that my life is now filled with doing the things that Jill and I want to do with family and friends.

That doesn't mean that I have lost the competitive edge that drove me on to scoring 100 first-class hundreds – far from it. I now play bridge three times a week at Edgbaston Golf Club, Moseley Bridge Club and Edgbaston Priory Lawn Tennis Club. And, as my regular Thursday partner, Jeff Bissenden, will confirm, while I always have fun, I enjoy myself just that little bit more when we win!

It is a passion that I share with Jill and our love of bridge goes back to the 1960s, when we first learned how to play the game on holiday with friends in Europe. From then on it became a regular pastime, particularly during County Championship matches when the game was interrupted by bad weather. The moment we got back into the pavilion, out came the cards, and Rohan Kanhai, Deryck Murray, John Jameson and I would sit down and play until the sun came out and we were summoned back onto the field of play.

On one occasion, in a match against Gloucestershire in Bristol, it rained solidly for three days. Not only did the four of us play bridge for three successive days in my hotel room, but we carried on throughout the night as well. Our absorption in the game was so intense that we never actually got around to unpacking our bags. As a consequence we arrived in Cardiff for the next match against Glamorgan totally exhausted, but were saved by more incessant rain which washed out another three days' play. Undeterred by the weather, however, Rohan, Deryck, John and I simply carried on with more rubbers of bridge.

Of decent club standard, I have won the odd competition along the way – a number of them with Jill, who has a much better grasp of the conventions and finer points of the game than me. Perhaps unsurprisingly, not all my bridge partners over the years have appreciated the quality of my game. I once played with Garry Sobers, for example, who was distinctly unimpressed by my approach. We had flown to Bangladesh to play a charity match to raise money for flood disaster relief. It rained for the entire week that we were there. In the absence of anything else to do, Rohan Kanhai, Donald Carr, Garry Sobers and I decided to play bridge. We also agreed that the losers would pay the winning pair £50 in prize money.

While I was delighted that my partner was Garry Sobers, I soon discovered that he played cards in the same adventurous, swashbuckling style in which he batted. His opening bids included such audacious calls as 'six spades' and 'seven no trumps'. Unsurprisingly, we were roundly defeated by Rohan and Donald, but far from reflecting on his grandiose bidding, Garry blamed me. 'I have to say, Dennis, man, you are the worst bridge player I've ever had as my partner. You were so bad, man, that you can pay my £25 share of the prize money.'

Although our bridge pairing ended up costing me £50, it was well worth it; to have had the greatest cricketer that God ever put breath into as my partner for that week in Bangladesh was undoubtedly the highlight of my card-playing career.

In addition to bridge, Jill and I also love playing golf, and for many years we have been members of Edgbaston Golf Club where, on the odd occasion, we have had success as a mixed pair in various events. I also play regularly with Roger Dancey, the former chief master of King Edward's School, Birmingham, and our partnership has also brought the occasional victory in both summer and winter foursomes.

Golf provides countless retired professional sportsmen and women with a physical outlet for their competitive instincts, and while I am now able to play three times a week in the summer – reducing to twice a week in the winter months – in my days as a professional cricketer, it was only on the rare Sundays that we had off that I was able to get out on the golf course. As a consequence, I was always keen to play when the opportunity arose, which is how I came to be part of one of cricket's longest golfing traditions.

Having begun in the early 1980s, Richie Benaud, Jack Bannister, Christopher Martin-Jenkins and Tony Lewis had established the practice of playing a foursomes match every year on the Friday of the Edgbaston

Test. On one occasion, however, Tony Lewis was unavailable and I was invited to play with Richie, Jack and CMJ.

After the game, when we were having breakfast, I suggested to Richie that it would be even more fun if they had a match against Edgbaston Golf Club. From then on, the press played a twelve-a-side foursomes match against EGC; the tee-off had to be at 6 a.m. to enable all the commentators and journalists to get to the ground to prepare for the day's play, and the losers were to pay for breakfast.

The fixture continued for the next three decades; for the first ten years the press team captain was Richie Benaud, who was followed for a similar period by CMJ. The duties were then shared for a further decade by the indomitable Ian 'Beefy' Botham and Mark Nicholas. Sadly, however, the tradition came to an end as the demands of modern broadcasting meant that the commentators had to get to the ground earlier and earlier.

Because opportunities to play golf were decidedly limited before my retirement, and because I started the game relatively late in life, the lowest handicap I ever got down to was 10 – a far cry from one of my cricketing heroes, Ted Dexter, who played off scratch. Just how good he was, however, only really became apparent on the 1962/63 Ashes tour of Australia when he was invited to play a round with Gary Player, one of the greatest golfers the world has seen. He was so impressed by Ted's game that he tried to persuade him to give up cricket and go with him to America to become a tournament professional. Ted turned the opportunity down as he felt that he would miss the camaraderie of being part of a team in which the pressure is also shared.

Having spent the first three years of my Test career learning how to handle pressure at the highest level, I have every sympathy with Ted's point of view. Playing golf for the sheer love of the game has given me a great deal of pleasure in my retirement, and while I am often frustrated by my inability to hit the ball as consistently sweetly as I would like, it is a relief to know that my livelihood does not depend on making par or getting a birdie on the next hole.

Above all, though, the main joy in retirement has been spending more time with Jill and the family. For the first fifteen or more years of Becca and Paul's lives, I hardly had a day at home during the summer, not to mention the extended periods away with England and MCC in the winter months. During those years Jill was effectively a single parent, and I have nothing but admiration and gratitude for the many ways in which she compensated for my absences.

What's more, the highs and lows of a professional sportsman's life are not easy to handle, and there were periods, even when at home, when poor performances made me distant and uncommunicative. Without Jill's understanding and support at such times I have no doubt that there would have been many more failures and fewer successes. Indeed, she deserves a medal for the love and loyalty she has given me for over fifty years. I am also indebted to her brother Jim and his wife Lyndon for their unfailing support.

Perhaps because of a deeply rooted need to atone for my absences as a husband and father, one of my main priorities since giving up my role at the ECB has been to devote far more time to Jill and our loving family which has, of course, expanded over the years and now includes Paul's beautiful wife Amanda Jayne – known as AJ – and our four delight- ful grandchildren: Becca's Hollie and Harry, and Paul and AJ's twins Charlotte – who we call 'Lottie' – and Grace, who goes by the name of 'Didi'.

Perhaps because I spent such prolonged periods away from home in past years, the times that I share with them now are far more precious than anything else in my life. That is not to say, however, that I would do anything different if I had my time again, and while I recognise the sacrifices that have been made because of my cricketing career, I am also immensely grateful for the rewards it has brought. In 1987, for example, on my retirement as a player, I was thrilled to be awarded an MBE for services to cricket because of my achievement in scoring 100 first-class hundreds.

Standing and waiting for the Queen to present me with the medal was every bit as nerve-racking as facing Dennis Lillee during the

1974/75 Ashes series. I could almost hear my heart beat as she walked towards me to present me with the medal. Having pinned the MBE insignia on my lapel and shaken my hand, she spoke: 'I understand that you have joined a very famous club,' she said.

For the life of me, I couldn't think which club she meant, and various possibilities flashed through my mind: Warwickshire County Cricket Club? Edgbaston Golf Club? The Primary Club? In total confusion I was unable to articulate any sort of reply, and so Her Majesty moved on to the next recipient of an award, wondering, perhaps, if all cricketers were quite so unresponsive!

I was also awarded an honorary doctorate by Birmingham University in 2007, following my retirement as chief executive of Warwickshire County Cricket Club. For someone who had left school aged 15 without any formal qualifications, it was a proud moment, and recognition that, for all my academic shortcomings, I had made a contribution to the city that has always been my home.

Along with all of this, in 2016 Birmingham City Council added my name to their 'Walk of Stars' on Broad Street in the city centre. Launched in 2007, it is the West Midlands equivalent of Hollywood's 'Walk of Fame' and is designed as a celebration of local people who have done the city proud. To have my name listed alongside such celebrities as Julie Walters, Lenny Henry, Jeff Lynne, Ann Haydon-Jones, Trevor Francis and Jasper Carrot never ceases to astonish me. The fact that the 1994 Warwickshire county cricket team is similarly honoured in recognition of winning the 'treble' makes me especially proud.

In the end, however, although I feel honoured and grateful for the accolades and awards that I have received over the years, what I cherish most in my retirement are the memories of the people, places and particular occasions that have left an indelible impression on me. And in the vast majority of cases, the moments that come back to me most often are filled with laughter.

After a day's play in a Test match at Lord's, for example, I was just making my way to the shower when the comedian Eric Morecambe came into our dressing room. Eager not to miss the opportunity of meeting him, I hurried my ablutions and came back into the room slightly damp and wearing no more than a towel around my waist. The moment the legendary comic saw my naked upper torso, he gripped my nipples between the thumb and forefinger of both hands. 'Light programme – home service,' he said, twiddling my nipples as if they were the knobs on a transistor radio. He then took a step back and, clocking that my chest was pretty hairy, added: 'My God, Amiss, you weren't born – you must have been trapped!'

While I now greatly enjoy the good humour and banter that are very much a part of playing bridge and golf, I do look back a little wistfully, from time to time, on the fun that I had on tour with my England teammates during the 1970s. The 'Saturday night club' that we introduced in India and Pakistan, for example, was a forum for fellowship and laughter. Central to the evening's entertainment was a dress code decided by members of the team in strict rotation. The result was that the attire chosen got ever more bizarre and scanty – one evening it included the wearing of nothing other than a jock-strap and socks, while on another occasion we were limited to pads and pants. The entertainment was entirely self-made and involved games such as charades, with Mike Brearley and Mike Selvey acting out obscure Russian novels like *The Brothers Karamazov* while Keith Fletcher and I attempted mimes of *Coronation Street* or *Crossroads*.

I doubt very much that such antics would be allowed in today's world of political correctness. While we enjoyed a relatively relaxed relationship with cricketing journalists – playing friendly rubbers of bridge, for example, with Peter Laker, John Thicknesse, Henry Blofeld and John Woodcock – modern players are subjected to intense scrutiny, not least through the numerous varieties of social media.

It is much harder now for modern players to let their hair down and have a night out as a team without drawing criticism from one quarter or another. In my view this is one of the very few sadnesses of the modern game. As a member of a team I felt that I was a part of something bigger and more important than myself, and it is that aspect of my long career in cricket that I miss most. Indeed, it is because of this that I am going to indulge myself by ending with the selection of 'My Best Warwickshire XI' and 'My Best England XI'.

In both cases, I have limited my choice to cricketers with whom I played. What's more, I have taken the unique opportunity of having sole and absolute authority for selection by picking myself for both sides. I'll leave others to decide if they agree or not, but, in the meantime, the eleven players I have chosen to represent 'My Best Warwickshire XI' are, in batting order:

1. Dennis Amiss
2. John Jameson
3. Rohan Kanhai
4. Alvin Kalicharan
5. MJK Smith (c)
6. Deryck Murray (wk)
7. Tom Cartwright
8. Brian McMillan
9. David Brown
10. Allan Donald
11. Lance Gibbs

Every one of the eleven players I have selected achieved international recognition, representing their respective countries in a combined total of 531 Test matches. Quite remarkably, however – particularly in view of the fact that my career overlapped with each member of the team – their first-class careers spanned a total of fifty-three years, from 1951, when MJK Smith made his debut for Leicestershire, to 2004, when Allan Donald finally retired from the game.

Although I have picked Deryck Murray, the great West Indian Test player, as the wicketkeeper, Geoff Humpage – a *Wisden* Cricketer of the Year in 1985 and an England One Day International star – would undoubtedly be my first-choice keeper in limited-over matches. With well over 1,000 dismissals and thirty-one centuries to his name in all forms of cricket, Geoff was a fine 'gloveman' and a match-winning middle-order batsman.

I have no doubt that if 'My Best Warwickshire XI' was able to compete in the County Championship and the various one-day competitions today, it would carry all before it, and bring the treble- and double-winning era of 1994 and 1995 back to Edgbaston.

While picking my Warwickshire side was a relatively simple exercise, deciding who to include and leave out of 'My Best England XI' required much more thought and deliberation. Should there be a place for Mike Brearley simply on the basis of his brilliant captaincy? Would I be able to justify the selection of Ian Botham having only played with him for England once, in a one-day international? How could I possibly omit batsmen of the calibre of John Edrich and Keith Fletcher? Would eyebrows be raised if I selected Bob Willis for 'My Best England XI' having left him out of my Warwickshire side?

In the end, all I could do was to take the bull by the horns and go with my instincts. The result was the selection of players who, in my view, had the technical skill, temperament and ambition to have won the 2019 Ashes series 4–0:

1. Dennis Amiss
2. Geoff Boycott
3. Graham Gooch (c)
4. Ken Barrington
5. Colin Cowdrey
6. Tom Graveney
7. Alan Knott (wk)
8. Ian Botham
9. John Snow
10. Derek Underwood
11. Bob Willis

The decision to select Bob Willis for my England XI, and not for Warwickshire, might appear controversial, but set in the context of the modern game it makes complete sense and I know that he would have agreed wholeheartedly. Indeed, he knew very early on in his Test career that if he tried to bowl at top speed throughout a County Championship season, he would not be fresh, fit and fired up when required by England. Like John Snow at Sussex, he only survived at the highest level because he was prepared to go into cruise-control mode when playing county cricket. As a result he avoided burn-out and became one of the greatest fast bowlers of all time. He was certainly on the list of stars that Kerry Packer wanted for World Series Cricket and – rumour has it – was on the verge of signing before changing his mind at the very last minute. It was a decision that may well have contributed to his appointment as England Captain a couple of years later. Bob's recent death at the age of only 70 will leave a huge gap in the lives of both his beloved family and the entire cricketing community.

Omitting Mike Brearley as captain of my England XI was one of the toughest calls, but in the end, the extraordinary quality of the batting line-up available outweighed the uniquely brilliant, analytical skills that Mike brought to the role of captaincy. Thus, I chose Graham Gooch as the skipper of the side even though I also included Colin Cowdrey in the eleven. This was primarily because the responsibility of leadership had a positive impact on Goochy's performance as a batsman. Indeed, while he was an even more prolific run scorer as skipper, there were occasions when Colin Cowdrey struggled for runs when he was captain.

There are, of course, some notable omissions from the team – not least Tony Greig, who was the fiercest competitor I ever played with. My selection of Ian Botham above him as the all-rounder might be seen as stretching the rules, as we played together for England in an ODI and not a Test match. They are, however, my rules to stretch, and Ian Botham – like Brian Lara and Garry Sobers – was the kind of match-winning, cricketing genius for whom regulations were made to be broken.

If I was selecting a touring party to represent England overseas, however, Greigy would undoubtedly be on the list, along with six other players who distinguished themselves at Test level during the ten years of my international career: John Edrich, the gritty and brave

Surrey left-hander – and also a member of the '100 Hundreds Club'; Keith Fletcher, who played 59 times for England, and one of the best players of spin bowling I have seen; Derek Randall, a brilliant fielder and a man for the big occasion who blasted his way to 174 in the Centenary Test in 1977; Bob Taylor, the most stylish and elegant of glovemen who would have been England's first-choice wicketkeeper in any other cricketing era; Basil D'Oliveira, a versatile and inspirational all-round cricketer whose Test career didn't begin until he was 35 years old; and Geoff Arnold, the best exponent of late swing and seam in the game.

To manage this extraordinarily gifted group of cricketers, I have chosen Ted Dexter. He is one of very few former players with the experience, personality and wisdom to command the respect of all. Along with Denis Compton, he is one of my cricketing heroes and it is a matter of real regret that, although I played against Ted in county cricket, his Test career had ended before mine began.

As I look back now on a career in cricket that spanned seven decades, the moment in April 1958 that I walked through the gates at Edgbaston, as a callow 15-year-old, on my first day as a professional cricketer, is as fresh in my memory as the occasion, at the end of the 2011 season, when Giles Clarke presented me with a beautiful silver cricket bat to mark my retirement as vice-chairman of the ECB. To have been so closely associated with the game I love for over half a century has been a privilege and a joy, but without the support and influence of a small group of people along the way none of it would have been possible.

I have already paid tribute to the roles that Tiger Smith, Derief Taylor and Tom Dollery played in helping me evolve as a cricketer in my early years. I have also highlighted the very significant influence that my close friends and cricketing colleagues David Brown, Tony Greig and Bob Woolmer had on my subsequent development from Test player to CEO. In addition, I was most fortunate, as CEO, to have the support of the Warwickshire committee led, during my time in the post, by two excellent chairmen: MJK Smith and Neil Houghton.

Aside from my coaches and cricketing colleagues, however, my life has been shaped and influenced by a small group of people whose commitment and support have been immeasurable. Indeed, I think of them as the trustees and the governing body of my life, and in this context Jill has undoubtedly been the chairman. Not only has she held our family together through the testing times of a cricketing widowhood, but she has been my best friend, most trusted adviser and advocate. Apart from the occasion at the Dorchester Hotel when I impetuously signed for Packer, I have discussed every important personal, family and professional decision with her, and the Lord only knows how many mistakes I'd have made along the way without her wise and considered counsel.

In my early years, it was my dad, Vic, and my Uncle Les who were the most significant influences in my life. While Dad was the person who first inspired my love of cricket, providing unfailing support and encouragement every step of the way, Uncle Les – who developed and expanded a highly successful tyre business before selling it to Dunlop – was a wonderful example of what could be achieved through hard work, determination and enterprise.

I am similarly indebted to my former business associates, Roger Hamilton-Brown and Howard Hodgson. In their different ways, they both gave me the business experience and acumen that enabled me to take on the chief executive role at Edgbaston. Without the opportunities and the backing that they provided, I could have ended my cricket career without aim or direction, and I will always be grateful for the trust and confidence that they had in my ability to succeed in business and commerce.

Another key influence in my life was Jack Bannister. As the senior professional at Warwickshire, I could not have asked for a better role model, nor a more supportive mentor, when I first joined the club. In his subsequent position as CEO of the Professional Cricketers' Association, of course, it was Jack's diplomacy and negotiating skills that saved my career when Warwickshire threatened to terminate my contract because I had signed for WSC. He was one of the most widely respected men in the game and his advice and friendship were invaluable.

My final 'trustee' is Keith Cook, my personal assistant as CEO at Edgbaston. Having worked in almost every department at Warwickshire County Cricket Club, Keith is a 'Bear' to the core of his being. Utterly discreet, dedicated and loyal, it was he who made sure that I was always in the right place, at the right time, with the right documentation. During moments of crisis, it was Keith who supported me, advised me and kept my blood pressure in check. Beloved by successive generations of Warwickshire cricketers, he continues to be indispensable in his current vital role of looking after the players' needs.

As former US President Woodrow Wilson said: 'Friendship is the only cement that will hold the world together', and as I look back over my life, while the memory of most of my 102 first-class hundreds is pretty sketchy, I have a vivid recollection of the many people, in addition to my family and trustees, who have played a significant role in my life: John Wright, my primary school teacher; John Oldham, Bernard Rowley, Roy McHenry and Ken Forsyth from my days at Smethwick Cricket Club; Bill Danter, Ken Stubbs and the Myring brothers from Olton Football Club; my regular bridge and golf partners, Jeff Bissenden and Roger Dancey; plus, of course, all our friends from Selly Park, Edgbaston and Harborne.

In my playing days I may well have been guilty of John Arlott's observation that, on the whole, 'we take life too lightly and sport too seriously'. Since retiring, however, I have begun to view things from a wider perspective and, in spite of Dennis Lillee and Jeff Thomson's best efforts, I can see that my life has been enormously blessed.

There have, of course, been trying times along the way and my life has not been without controversy. As a 'double rebel' – joining Kerry Packer and the much-criticised South African tour – I was 'Public Enemy Number One' as far as the cricketing establishment, the media and several of my county colleagues were concerned. In recent times, there has been some pressure to 'name and shame' those who sent me to Coventry when I returned from WSC. There have also been suggestions that I should 'out' the person who was really responsible for bringing drugs into the Warwickshire dressing room. I have, however, always preferred conciliation to finger pointing; besides which, time has moved on and so have I.

Cricket, too, has changed dramatically over the seven decades of my involvement in the game, and I make no apology for saying that 99 per cent of the developments have been for the better. In my view, cricket is now far better placed to meet the challenges of the modern world than it was when I first became a professional player. Moreover, when people ask me to identify the single most important factor in bringing about this transformation, I always point to Kerry Packer and WSC as being the catalyst for much-needed change.

Thus, although I ended my career proud to be part of cricket's establishment, I have never quite lost the spirit of adventure or the instinct to rebel. Perhaps this explains why, while so many players of my generation have a deep and nostalgic attachment to 'the good old days', I admire the spirit of innovation that is central to the future of the game that has done me proud.

A Postscript: COVID, Captain Tom and Crawley

On 16 March 2020 – just a few days before this book was due to go to the printers – the UK Government announced the 'COVID Lockdown' that changed all our lives drastically. Having been born in the shadow of the Second World War, I am only too aware that it is at times of national emergency that heroes come to the fore. The crisis that coronavirus generated was no exception.

In the midst of deep anxiety and fear, our spirits were lifted by war veteran Captain Tom Moore, who raised more than £32 million for the National Health Service by walking endless laps of his garden just weeks prior to his 100th birthday. What an inspiration! But it wasn't just his actions that were so uplifting; every word he spoke was filled with optimism. In one BBC interview, for example, he delivered the simplest of messages:

Please always remember tomorrow will be a good day.

Weighed down as we were in March and early April by an endless succession of gloomy statistics about infection rates, hospital admissions and fatalities, Captain Tom gave us a much-needed reason to smile and, perhaps more importantly, a lost sense of what really matters.

In cricketing terms, listening to Captain Tom articulate his 'can-do' philosophy was every bit as inspiring as watching Viv Richards, Gary

Sobers or Brian Lara walk out to bat. It didn't matter that a wicket had just fallen when they made their way to the crease. Just as Captain Tom believes in looking forward to the good that is coming rather than dwell on past disappointments, so the greats of sport banish negative thoughts from their minds when they enter their chosen arena.

Since the beginning of the pandemic Jill and I have done our best to keep Captain Tom's example in the forefront of our minds. What excuse could there be for me to sit idle at the tender age of 77 whilst the remarkable Captain Tom – twenty-three years my senior – walks yet another lap of his garden?

In spite of the lockdown, Jill and I have continued to play golf and bridge, even though it meant a bit of improvisation. Before the golf club opened in May, for example, we were fortunate enough to be able to hit a few balls (off a playing mat, of course!) on the KES Birmingham playing fields, which we can access via a gate from our back garden. And, as far as bridge is concerned, lockdown has drawn me out of the technological dark ages: Jill and I have been playing online with friends as far away as Malta.

There have been new things as well: the empty roads of March and April encouraged me to use my electric bicycle far more than in the past and, more recently, I have discovered the joys of cooking. Indeed, I am now a member of two men's cooking groups and we take it in turns to select a dish and share photographs of our efforts with each other.

Beyond that, however, Captain Tom has inspired us to do whatever we can to support others in the community, those who don't have partners or gardens or enjoy the benefit of good health. It was because of this that – along with the Warwickshire County Cricket Club playing staff – I was pleased to be part of an initiative that involved ringing club members to check that they were alright. I also got involved in a campaign led by the administrative team at Edgbaston to raise money for the Birmingham hospitals. Following the example of the 2.6 Challenge, which was launched on 26 April, the day the London Marathon should have been staged, I had to engage in an activity based around the number 2.6 or 26, complete the challenge and then donate or fundraise to support a chosen charity. Much to the amusement of friends and family, it was Jill who came up with the idea that I should swap golfing gear for a pinafore and do twenty-six consecutive days of household chores!

Looking back now on lockdown and the summer that followed I am struck not only by the sense of community and camaraderie that was evident, but also by the purposeful ingenuity shown in so many different areas. What's more, I was especially proud that cricket led the way in providing some much-needed entertainment.

All credit to the West Indies and Pakistan cricket squads for coming to the UK in such uncertain times. We should also acknowledge the role played by the ECB's administrators; not always noted for imagination or creative thinking, they found a safe and successful solution to staging international competition in extraordinarily difficult circumstances. It is a testament to the skill and competitive enthusiasm of the players that, in spite of crowdless grounds, there was no shortage of excitement or drama, and the quality of the cricket was exceptional. This was exemplified by the continuing achievements of Jimmy Anderson and Stuart Broad who reminded us – if indeed, we needed reminding – that age is no barrier to success. The highlight of the summer, though, was the emergence of Zak Crawley as an international Test cricketer of the highest pedigree. At just 22 years old, his 267 against Pakistan at Southampton is the second-highest maiden century by an England batsman and the seventh-highest overall. His elegance and effortless timing reminded me of the great Peter May and, just as he was, I believe Zak Crawley will be the finest player of his generation.

Closer to home, Warwickshire bade farewell to Ian Bell, who announced his retirement after twenty-one years in the game. With 114 Test Matches, 22 Test centuries and 140 One Day Internationals to his name, Ian has been one of England and Warwickshire's most distinguished players. A naturally gifted stroke maker, his magnificent cover drive will be much missed at Edgbaston.

As far as the 2020 county cricket season was concerned, I was delighted that the amended championship format was named after my old teammate Bob Willis, who sadly died in December 2019. Bob would have thoroughly approved of the competition, which has three regionalised groups that consist of six teams per group. Perhaps the structure of the 2020 Bob Willis Trophy is the way forward, as it gives every county club a chance of winning the championship. Perhaps the future will be even more radical, with fewer counties playing four-day cricket and the others competing in limited-overs competition. Whatever the future holds, I'm of the Captain Tom school of philosophy: 'tomorrow will be a good day.'

Appendix

The Statistics of DLA's Batting Career

Test Cricket							
Matches	Innings	Not Out	Runs	HS	Ave	50s	100s
50	88	10	3,612	262★	46.30	11	11
One-Day Internationals							
Matches	Innings	Not Out	Runs	HS	Ave	50s	100s
18	18	0	859	137	47.72	1	4
First-Class Cricket							
Matches	Innings	Not Out	Runs	HS	Ave	50s	100s
658	1,139	126	43,423	262★	42.86	212	102
List A Matches							
Matches	Innings	Not Out	Runs	HS	Ave	50s	100s
404	391	34	12,519	137	35.06	77	15

Index